Philadelphia ❧
An American Paris

Paris? Mais, non, chérie; c'est Philadelphie!

Philadelphia
An American Paris

Joseph L. Borkson

CAMINO BOOKS, INC. *Philadelphia*

To Marilyn and Dan, Pearl and Elliot

Printed in China

1 2 3 4 5 04 03 02

Library of Congress Cataloging-in-Publication Data

Borkson, Joseph L.
      Philadelphia : an American Paris / Joseph L. Borkson.
              p. cm.
Includes bibliographical references.
      ISBN 0-940159-71-6
  1. Philadelphia (Pa.)—Pictorial works. 2. Philadelphia (Pa.)—Description and travel.
3. Philadelphia (Pa.)—Civilization. 4. Paris (France)—Description and travel. 5. Paris (France)—Civilization. 6. United States—Civilization—French influences. I. Title.
      F158.37 .B67 2001
      974.8'11—dc21

      2001003868

Cover and interior design: Adrianne Onderdonk Dudden

Unless otherwise noted, all photographs are courtesy of Joseph L. Borkson.

This book is available at a special discount on bulk purchases for promotional, business, and educational use. For information write to:

Publisher
Camino Books, Inc.
P.O. Box 59026
Philadelphia, PA 19102

www.caminobooks.com

Contents

High Hollow (Chestnut Hill)

Acknowledgments

The publication of a color photo essay book in today's world is nothing short of a small miracle. The initial expense involved in producing such a work without any guarantee of salability requires a great deal of commitment from a great many people and a good measure of luck. Because of this, I am indebted to so many who have helped me accomplish this small miracle.

First and foremost, I am grateful to my publisher, Mr. Edward Jutkowitz of Camino Books. His enthusiasm for the project and his patience with my ongoing "ideas" were the ties which brought it all together. And to Michelle Scolnick at Camino, a special note of thanks.

To Madame Danièle Thomas-Easton, the Honorary Consul of France in Philadelphia and Wilmington, I am deeply grateful. Her ever-present help with the proofreading and her passion for my photos pushed me forward at times when I might have taken an unproductive path. By the way, her Gallic enthusiasm for the project was always a special delight to me which I could never translate into the idiom.

To the family of Haym Solomon here in Philadelphia, I am especially grateful. Dr. Tereza Solomon-DeMoody, whose great ancestor realized a special service to his new country in helping to finance our

American Revolution before the French alliance, was a constant source of support and devotion when I felt alone and up against insurmountable odds. Thank you, Tereza.

To Dr. Jean-Pierre Garnier, CEO of GlaxoSmithKline, my heartfelt admiration and appreciation. His personal review of the manuscript and his warmhearted support were the springboard which made others begin to sit up and take notice.

To my agent, Ms. Jodie Rhodes, a special note of gratitude. In the shark-infested waters of book publication, Jodie's commitment was nothing short of an obsession to find a publisher for my efforts, and I find it difficult to express the emotion I feel toward her for the gargantuan effort she made to realize this dream of mine.

To all the familiar faces at Ritz Camera Shops who put up with my "nagging" toward the special vision I had in the development and reproduction of the thousands of pictures of an American Paris: Big Greg, Chris and Cindy, Tami, Linda, Rick and Dave; I cannot forget Dave. Thanks to all of you.

To all my friends at Taws Artist Supplies on Walnut Street: Ron, Pat, Mark and so many others, thank you. Whatever I wanted to do, the good people at Taws were always there to give their all to bring it together.

To two special friends who proofread the manuscript and gave me inestimable guidance as only two old friends could do: Mr. Robert Tree and Mr. Robert Warshaw.

To the memory of Mr. Leo C. Coleman, Jr., a native of my hometown of Jacksonville, Florida, who came to love Philadelphia and to call it home as much as I. His faith helped me through a difficult period in my medical residency here in Philadelphia.

To so many countless friends and patients whose excitement and encouragement pushed me to greater heights, thank you.

Foreword

*P*utting this book together was truly a labor of love for me. Philadelphia has such incomparable beauty and so much American history that I could ramble until my final days and still discover "new" finds which would cause my spirits to soar. And I never knew this before moving here in the early '80s. This may sound a bit presumptuous, but I doubt that anyone, native or transplant, knows all the rich, hidden beauties of this great city. This book is an attempt to point out some of these beauties that a visitor to the city might never know and to revel in the celebration of an American city which rivals the elegance of the European capitals.

There was good reason for Philadelphia's ascent to become the foremost city of the country during those tough, formative years of the Revolution and thereafter. Even though New York and Boston predate the founding of Philadelphia by almost a hundred years, it was here in the Quaker City that the highest ideals of what we think of as being American came to establish themselves. Here, the Quaker values of honesty and fair play, tolerance and industriousness brought about something unique in the American experience—a city with a true sense of community. The local Indians were treated with respect and dealt with fairly. The Quakers were the first group in the colonies to decry the evils of slavery. In fact, it was a young Frenchman, Anthony Benezet, who arrived with his family in

Fenêtre avec des plantes (Chestnut Hill)

the early 1730s, left his father's mercantile business and began to exercise his benevolence by establishing the African School and by teaching in the Friends' English School. His social philosophy mirrored that of his compatriots in the new ideas of the Enlightenment which were beginning to take shape in his homeland. In 1758, Benjamin Franklin persuaded a group of philanthropic Englishmen to open a school for blacks under the reverend of Christ Church.

The colonial city also served as a haven for those peoples who suffered persecution in other parts of the Americas. Indians, Acadians (French Canadians), blacks, Catholics, Jews—they all came under the protection of Quaker tolerance.

In the 17th and 18th centuries, both England and France were coming into their own as centralized powers under their respective sovereigns; but it was in France under Louis XIV that absolutism reached its zenith. Versailles, Louis's monument to this absolutism, reflects the Sun King's control not only over his people, but also over nature. The area to the southwest of Paris that Louis designated for his Versailles to be built was essentially marshland. Mountains of earth had to be carted in to build up the land around the palace; fully grown trees were uprooted from forests fifty to one hundred miles away; and gardens, perfectly trimmed, against a backdrop of gilded baroque fountains were all created as if the king's will were all it took to transform a swamp into one of the most magnificent settings the world has come to know. Louis actually delighted in this challenge to Nature and he intended this rich display, like the founding of the Royal Academies of the Arts and Architecture at this same time, to graphically portray the power and glory of France to the rest of the world. At the height of construction there were more than 36,000 laborers working on his beloved Versailles. Upon his death in 1715, however, the French people began to manifest a yearning for liberty which categorically rejected this absolutism of so many years and paralleled the developing yearnings for liberty of the American colonists. The authors of the Enlightenment—Montesquieu, Rousseau, Voltaire and John Locke—were the spokesmen for the people and reflected the people's yearnings for their individual freedom.

To the British, the colonies represented a business and a place to unload their dissidents. To the majority of the French, however, America was a noble experiment which had its resonance in the ideals of their Enlightenment. Liberty was the ephemeral concept which joined the two peoples spiritually.

While it was unquestionably a bitter fate to be poor and a peasant during the 17th and 18th centuries in either "merrie ole England" or "*la douce France*," the French peasants shared an attachment to the land which transcended any politics. The voluptuousness of the French countryside is an enchantment that even foreigners today are drawn to. Not just to her monuments or to the beauty of her landscape, for the *joie de vivre* of France captivates the visitor with things from everyday life: her produce, her food, her art, her intellectual curiosity, her diversity, even the sing-song quality of her language. Is it any wonder that fewer French than British chose to emigrate to the Americas? It was not so hard to leave the oppression of England, but to leave France . . . well, that was a tough thing to do.

There is a misconception among many peoples of the world that Britain was a stronger power than France and, therefore, the greater colonizer of the two powers. The truth, however, lies in the above. Militarily, France was England's match, even though the "sceptered isle" could boast naval superiority at certain periods of history. This is why the two powers were such bitter rivals during the two centuries in which America was beginning to take shape.

France is our oldest ally and partner in the cause of liberty. She has always helped us, inspired us and captivated us as Americans; and nowhere in our country is her stamp of grace more evident than here in Philadelphia. While this book deals with the art, architecture and culture of France in the city, there is an underlying leitmotif for a mutual love of liberty as shared by our two countries.

Joseph L. Borkson

Introduction

Philadelphia has long been synonymous with American history, and rightfully so. It was here in the Graff house at the corner of Seventh and Market Streets that a young Thomas Jefferson conceived the wording which became the Declaration of Independence in June 1776; and here in the Pennsylvania State House, later to be called Independence Hall, that the document was signed the following month on July 4th by the representatives of the thirteen colonies.

It was also here that the battles of the Brandywine and Germantown were fought at the onset of the Revolutionary War, and in that terrible winter of 1777–78, the British headquartered in Philadelphia while General Washington encamped with the beleaguered Continental army twenty-five miles to the west at Valley Forge.

The Articles of Confederation, which gave some semblance of cohesiveness to the colonies; the Constitutional conventions, which argued and finally ratified the famous document that still frames our country's legal code—all these momentous political events took place in Philadelphia. It was only natural that the city serve as the national capital when the new country came together under Constitutional law.

But there is another side to this historic place which very few

Mr. Jefferson actually posed for this marble bust by Jean Antoine Houdon, perhaps the finest sculptor of the day.
George Nixon Black Fund.
Courtesy of Museum of Fine Arts, Boston. © 2000 Museum of Fine Arts, Boston. All Rights Reserved.

tourists get a chance to see, a side which may be the biggest surprise of all. Philadelphia, I have discovered to my amazement since moving here in 1983, is an elegant, strikingly beautiful city which rivals the beauty of the European capitals; yes, even the beauty of the "City of Lights" herself—Paris. In my walks around the city I have often marveled at how similar the scenery along the banks of the Schuylkill is to that on the banks of the Seine. And, upon reflection, there is good reason for this.

At the time of the Revolution and into the 19th century, Philadelphia was our country's largest city. Her resources and her close connections with Europe, especially France, have endowed her with a French flavor which is everywhere. From the fascination of Franklin and Jefferson with French art and culture and the strength of our first great ally in the fight for independence, to the elegant Empire style of Napoléon, which greatly stimulated the Greek Revival in American arts and architecture, to the lavish use of the mansard roof and the modified classicism of the Second Empire of Napoléon III and the subsequent, pervasive influence of the École des Beaux Arts, France has truly been an inspiration to the arts in America, and most especially, in Philadelphia. This is why I think of Philadelphia as an American Paris. Yet it is greatly surprising how long this unique, elegant aspect of our fair city has gone unsung and unappreciated in the many tourist guides. Even more surprising is that no professional writer or photographer has picked up on this uncanny connection, for when I sought out background material for the striking French influence on the art and architecture in Philadelphia, there was little to be had.

Rowing on the Schuylkill

*P*hiladelphia was founded on the highest ideals of the American experience. Designed on a grid to facilitate commerce and industry, founded on the freedom of religious conviction, initially populated by a skilled and industrious group of colonists, secured by peaceful negotiations with the local Indian tribes, supported by the richest farmland to be found in any American colony and situated on the banks of a navigable river to promote trade, Philadelphia became, within the first hundred years after its founding in 1682, the largest, wealthiest and most beautiful city in the colonies. William Penn, our noble founder, had envisioned a city which would not only be prosperous, but one which would strive for the highest human values of brotherhood and one which would be different from all the other cities of the world. Hence the name, Philadelphia, the Greek term for "brotherly love." Initially a refuge for his Quaker brethren who were

This childlike rendering of William Penn and his Quaker contingency negotiating with the Indians is by American artist Edward Hicks. It is also in the style of Henri Rousseau; and like both artists' famous themes of "The Peaceable Kingdom," there is a distinct feeling of peaceful coexistence.

so persecuted in England and Germany, Penn's "towne on the Delaware" also stood for religious tolerance of all sects, Christian and non-Christian. In a like manner, he made no provision for garrisons or standing militias, as the Indians had been placated through respect and peaceful negotiations; and he made no provision for any specific municipal government, as he wanted to liberate his town from the political factionalism which plagued so many of the European towns and cities. He quite literally believed in the mutual advantages of peace and prosperity and wanted to give his new town

Our founder (William Penn)

every chance to develop in that direction. But Penn's legacy to Philadelphia had an even greater, far-reaching effect in his commitment to the public good. His first priority always seemed to reflect a sense of community, which is often attributed to his Quaker point of view.

In the 17th and early 18th centuries, before the advent of industrialism and manufacturing, a town's prosperity depended on trade. Cities grew as focal points for trade; and trade, for its part, was dependent on the capacity to transport goods in and out. The great rivers and tributaries served as the first highways in this commerce. Penn understood this pivotal aspect in the growth of the city and protected the mile-long Delaware waterfront by refusing to grant permanent ownership to anyone. He even charged a special rent, called a "quitrent," to those who profited from the use of the waterfront, and put the money into the development of the western sectors of the city which extended to the Schuylkill. By doing this, he avoided monopoly and attempted to provide his new city with a sense of order and direction. For even though Philadelphia became as big and as prosperous as it did in those first hundred years of development, it is uncanny that the Graff house at Seventh and Market Streets, where Jefferson composed the Declaration of Independence, was still considered "west" of the more populated section of the city in 1776, and it was located just one block from the Pennsylvania State House. The city had actually grown in a densely populated arc along the Delaware riverfront. Penn had foreseen these trends and in his original plan of 1683, he judiciously outlined the city with the incorporation of four square parks in the four sectors and a central public square: these parks—Franklin Square, Washington Square, Rittenhouse Square and Logan Square, together with Centre Square in the middle—still bear the same locations as originally set forth by him.

This larger sense of community, this coupling of wealth and public responsibility, also manifested itself in the business community with the enforcement of standard weights and measures and the outlawing of usury by setting an upper limit for interest rates of 8 percent. Business principles seemed to be dictated by Quaker values of honesty and fair play, and these principles spilled over into government as well.

Although Philadelphia was established well after other urban centers along the eastern seaboard, it was here that this sense of community fostered the founding of the country's first public library, the first hospital, the first art museum, the first zoo, the first volunteer fire company, the first public school and many other firsts too numerous to mention. And the aim of William Penn to promote the greater good of the community, while at the same time encouraging personal industriousness, has imbued the city's spirit, yielding a long list of Philadelphians from Penn's time to the present who have become prosperous and have given back to the city in the most generous and humanitarian ways. Is it any wonder why the new towns springing up in the West, from the Ohio Basin to the Great Lakes, took Philadelphia as their model city with its orderly street-grid, its language, its social customs and its cultural trends, rather than the cities of New England or the Old South?

Philadelphia continued to grow rapidly into the 19th century and to transform itself from a trading center into a manufacturing and industrial center. New York, because of the greater accessibility of its harbor, and the diminishing naval threat from Great Britain after the War of 1812, began to surpass Philadelphia in terms of population after 1810, but Philadelphia continued to remain the definitive economic, political and social force in the country throughout most of the 19th century. Philadelphia's harbor was a good one, but the trip up the Delaware could be hazardous without prior knowledge of the channels and shoals, and the trip added an additional 200 miles to the overall voyage from Europe. Paradoxically, this served the city well in earlier times because the harbor's entrance could be defended against invaders by sea. While preparing this book, I found it particularly interesting to learn how the colonists attempted to defend Philadelphia's harbor after the Declaration of Independence was issued. Their fear, of course, was the possibility of a British naval attack on the city from the Delaware River; and at the time, the British navy had the most powerful armada on the seas.

The basic plan, which may have been devised by Ben Franklin, was to place so-called *chevaux-de-frise* (wooden horses) with protruding spikes of iron in the main channels below the city; these protruding spikes gave a "frizzy" look to the wooden structures to which they were attached, not unlike horses' manes. This ingenious ploy, it was hoped, would deter any unfriendly ship from coming up the river and would give the paltry forces on the riverbanks some type of advantage. This "David and Goliath" tactic demonstrates the Yankee ingenuity sorely needed at the time and shows how hard-pressed the Americans were for war matériel in comparison to the British. Had it not been for men like Robert Morris and Haym Solomon, who helped to finance the Revolution before the French alliance, the scenario would have been even worse. Amazingly, the "frizzy horses" seemed to work! When General Howe finally approached Philadelphia with the British forces in August 1777, he decided to sail up the Chesapeake Bay and proceed overland to reach the city.

By 1800, Philadelphia had become a pretty city of red-brick houses trimmed in white and framed in a tree-lined checkerboard. The streets from east to west—that is, the streets running from the Delaware to the Schuylkill—were named after the local trees: Chestnut, Walnut, Locust, Pine, Spruce, and the numbered streets from north to south cut across these at right angles with Front, Second, Third and so on, in ascending order from the Delaware waterfront. A visitor to the city would easily be able to orient himself, and commerce could be facilitated through this sense of order and regularity. The two wide avenues of the town would intersect at the public square (Centre Square) in the middle of this grid; these were High Street, later changed to Market Street, running east to west, and Broad Street, appropriately named, as the north-south thoroughfare. How many towns in this country have a rectilinear street pattern with their streets named after the local trees?

Up to 1800, Philadelphia had witnessed the construction of a goodly number of handsome Georgian and Federal-style houses and government buildings, which gave it a decidedly English appearance. This is not surprising since Pennsylvania had been a British colony only twenty-five years before. But after 1800, the city began to develop in a different direction. From this time on, even though English styles continued to play an integral part in our 19th-century architecture, it was the French influence which was to predominate in bringing an elegant, exuberant look to the city which, to me, is so strikingly beautiful and so European at the same time. But before going further, let me make a little historical digression.

No country in our history has given more to the American cause than France. While England was setting the stage with her rich heritage of language, culture and common law, France was the kindred spirit giving spark to the cause.

In 1715, Louis XIV, *le roi soleil* ("the sun king"), had finally breathed his last and with his passing, the divine right of kings with its unquestioned authority produced its most dramatic reaction in 18th-century France with the ideals of the Enlightenment. When Thomas Jefferson stated that "every man has two countries, his own and France," he was dramatically referring to these new social and political ideas of the Enlightenment, sometimes called the "Age of Voltaire" after its most famous proponent. In brief, these ideas rebuked the authoritarianism of the state and the church and proclaimed the innate rights of the individual to freedom. Our Declaration of Independence and Constitution are based on these ideas of the Enlightenment as understood by our Founding Fathers.

In 1777, Benjamin Franklin of Philadelphia became our first minister to the Court of Versailles; his job was to forge the French alliance with the young American republic. At this point, we may have already declared our independence, but no one had taken us too seriously; this was still an "internal colonial affair" to be resolved by Philadelphia and London. To the French people, however, including the intellectuals of the noble class, Franklin was taken to be the model American—philosopher, inventor, a self-made man. To them, he was the epitome of the Enlightenment, and their alignment with him had its roots in a mutual passion for liberty and self-determination. He hardly needed to speak at all as our ambassador; the recognition of his identification with the French people and their

Mr. Franklin at the Court of Versailles

struggle for liberty was the tableau on which the alliance finally became a reality in February 1778. Of course, the French wanted to diminish the might of their most fearsome adversary; of course, they wanted to secure certain trade agreements with the new republic; of course, they wanted to make fairly certain that the Americans could win, first of all, and, secondly, would refrain from making a separate peace with England after taking French aid. But political maneuverings aside, on hearing the news of the brave stand the Americans made at Germantown and the British defeat at Saratoga, both in 1777, the French agreed to the alliance. To the Continentals fighting back home, this alliance with France would rank with the final British surrender at Yorktown as the two great, spiritual high points in the war. The alliance, in effect, legitimized the American republic, and the Americans began to feel pride for the first time as citizens of their new country which had just become recognized by the most powerful nation in Europe. The surrender at Yorktown was a combined Franco-American effort, as well, with the Comte de Rochambeau in charge of the French naval forces.

It is certainly no secret that France was heavily into deficit spending during the reign of Louis XVI, which had commenced in 1774; we all know the vignette of his wife, Marie Antoinette, exhorting the Parisian people to have a little cake during the riots caused by the bread shortages. The point here is that France went even more deeply into debt with the financing of the American Revolution, and the unwillingness of the aristocracy to help with the ever-increasing tax burden endured by the French masses was a major wound which would catalyze the events leading to their own revolution in 1789. *Liberté, égalité, fraternité!* The Enlightenment inspired the American Revolution which, in turn, gave momentum to the French Revolution—the three phenomena stand out to characterize the 18th century—and all three were intimately connected in substance and in spirit.

With the idea exchange came the cultural exchange: the flower of

French nobility, imbued by the ideals of the Enlightenment and patriotism, came to fight side by side with the Americans, the young Marquis de Lafayette, not quite twenty years old, among them. Notable French émigrés, fleeing the Reign of Terror in revolutionary France, also came to America and, later, more émigrés arrived during the Napoleonic wars. And where did these French émigrés disembark? Yes, they came to Philadelphia. André Michaux, the French botanist, said that Philadelphia in 1800 was "the most extensive, the handsomest and the most populous city in the United States." Jean Jacques Audubon, Eleuthère Irénée du Pont, Joseph and Lucien Bonaparte, Charles Maurice de Talleyrand, Pierre Duponceau, Michael Bouvier (great-great-grandfather to Jackie O.), Stephen Girard and Anthony Benezet were among the better-known of these French émigrés. Thanks to such Francophiles as Franklin, Jefferson, Robert Morris and Nicholas Biddle, and French chroniclers like the Marquis de Chastellux, Moreau de St. Méry, Châteaubriand, de Tocqueville and Crèvecœur, French culture found itself solidly ensconced in Philadelphia at the beginning of the 19th century.

In the Napoleonic period, during the first fifteen years of the 19th century, there arose a renewed interest in the monumental Greco-Roman and Egyptian styles in the arts and architecture. Napoléon wanted to dignify his reign by way of the dramatic and eternal emotion conjured up by the classical arts and architecture and to visibly show the world the glory and grandeur of France by making Paris the most beautiful of cities. His Empire style of architecture and furniture aimed at strength and sublimity rather than grace of relief or charm of detail. Through the patronage and influence of the French émigrés, this Empire style translated itself into American furniture and architecture, and produced distinguished examples here in Philadelphia. The Second National Bank on Chestnut Street and Founders' Hall at Girard College on Girard Avenue are the most striking examples of this period; Nicholas Biddle's country seat of Andalusia on the banks of the Delaware, just above the Northeast section of the city, almost duplicates his office address in appearance. He was president of the Second National Bank.

Founders' Hall on the campus of Girard College merits a special mention here. When Charles Dickens visited Philadelphia in 1842, he wrote that "near the city is a most splendid unfinished marble

The Second National Bank of the United States of America

Founders' Hall (Girard College)

structure for the Girard College, founded by a deceased gentleman of that name and of enormous wealth, which, if completed according to the original design, will be perhaps the richest edifice of modern times." He was not exaggerating; in its stark, classic simplicity, it is, to me, the most dramatic building in Philadelphia and one of the most dramatic I have ever seen. No description or picture can really do it justice; it must be seen to appreciate the awesome and harmonious presence it projects. A Greek Revival building of massive Corinthian columns crowned with a triangular pediment, this elegant edifice took its inspiration from the Church of the Madeleine in Paris; but I must admit that Founders' Hall, with its particular location, can easily be overlooked. By the way, the Church of the Madeleine was probably not intended as a church when its foundations were laid early in Napoléon's reign, and it was not completed until 1842.

Founders' Hall (Girard College)

Founders' Hall, which was begun in 1833 and completed in 1847, is the main building on the campus of Girard College. When I first moved to Philadelphia, my daily commute along Girard Avenue past the campus, with its main entrance at 20th Street, failed to draw my attention to the Hall, which I later found so hard to believe. My pre-occupation with the trolley tracks and potholes along the avenue and a high wall surrounding the school precluded all but a few seconds' glance into the main entrance for a brief appreciation of the glorious buildings within. Founders' Hall was designed by Thomas Ustick Walter and Nicholas Biddle. Walter, who was one of America's greatest architects, also helped Biddle remodel his home, Andalusia, on the banks of the Delaware in the Greek Revival style. His fame, however, rested not on any of his buildings in Philadelphia, but on his design for the magnificent new Capitol dome in Washington, D.C., along with the wings for the Senate and the House of Representatives.

Nicholas Biddle's "Andalusia" on the Delaware

Stephen Girard (1750–1831), the founder of Girard College, was one of those Philadelphians whose memory is as much a part of the city's legacy as that of any of her monuments. At the age of 14, he left his home in Bordeaux to serve as a cabin boy on a ship trading in the French West Indies. By 1776, he had become captain and part-owner of a ship bound for New York which had come under British blockade at the beginning of the War of Independence. In order to escape, Girard brought his ship up the Delaware to Philadelphia, sold his interest in it and opened a small business on Water Street. At the age of 43, he had still not risen to the heights his business acumen would take him, but he came to the rescue of many Philadelphians who had succumbed to the yellow fever epidemic of 1793. At a time when most Philadelphians, both rich and poor, were trying to escape the horror of the epidemic and the Pennsylvania Hospital and Almshouse refused to receive plague victims for fear of endangering their other patients, Girard helped to organize the Bush Hill estate of Andrew Hamilton, which the city had taken over to house the many citizens affected by the fever. With the help of Peter Helm, a local cooper, he took charge of Bush Hill and transformed it from a dirty, stench-ridden hell-hole with patients wallowing in their own vomit and excrement into a clean, airy hospital which gave hope as well as medical attention to the desperately sick victims of the epidemic. He also enlisted the aid of a French physician, Dr. Jean Devèze, as supervisor of Bush Hill. Moving a French physician in as supervisor past the city's medical establishment, which still treated the fever victims with bleeding and purges, was probably an accomplishment that only Girard could manage. As it turned out, the move was pivotal as well as fortuitous. The French physicians had had more experience in dealing with these epidemics and their special approach to hygiene and the use of cool liquids, cool baths and mild medicines saved many lives.

After the epidemic had passed, Philadelphia entered an era of prosperity as a busy port and the national capital, and Girard grew exceedingly wealthy in the worldwide trade which was to follow. He became the owner of a fleet of clipper ships named after the great French philosophers of the Enlightenment, including *le Montesquieu*, *le Rousseau* and *le Voltaire*, and traded extensively in Northern Europe, China and the Far East; Chinese markets were beginning to develop because of the great demand for tea, silk and porcelains. And, along with this worldwide trading, shrewd investments in land and mines increased his fortune. By 1811, when the First National Bank's charter had been revoked by the U.S. Congress, Girard bought the august building on Third Street and founded the Girard Trust Company. The failure of Congress to renew the Bank's charter in 1811 deprived the U.S. Treasury of a means to raise funds so that the government had to resort to a $5 million federal bond issue in order to pay the costs of the ongoing war with Great Britain, of which the American public was only able to come up with $200,000; it was Stephen Girard, together with his friend John Jacob Astor, who stepped in to finance the balance so that Girard, in great part, actually financed the War of 1812. On his death in 1831, he had become the wealthiest man in the country. Girard College—*collège* in the French sense of the word—was intended as a boarding school for fatherless boys aged 10 to 18, but to me his legacy goes far beyond the material gifts he bestowed. His compassion for his fellow Philadelphians and his fearlessness in the face of personal risk during the yellow fever epidemic of 1793; his courage to buck the medical establishment by enlisting the expertise of those physicians who might be better able to deal with the horrible suffering; his constant devotion to his wife, who spent many years in an insane asylum before her death; his forward-thinking business practice of generously sharing the profits of his trading ventures with the captains of his ships; even the portraits he had commissioned of the Chinese merchants with whom he had dealt in the Orient—all these images of Stephen Girard give testimony to a man of flesh and blood and a very special Philadelphian, as well as a very special American.

*D*uring the era of the Second Empire in France from the early 1850s through 1870, classicism again took center stage, but with it came the "Mansard Madness" of roof design that spread throughout the city in every type of building. Although this classicism had been modified to offer more detail through design and sculpture, it still maintained the order, proportion and symmetry of the French Renaissance. The most notable examples of the Second Empire style are City Hall at the intersection of Broad and Market Streets and Memorial Hall in Fairmount Park, two of the most prominent and noteworthy buildings in Philadelphia.

In 1853, Emperor Napoléon III engaged Georges Haussmann to further beautify Paris by a giant urban renewal project which developed broad, straight avenues; elegant, newly styled classical buildings with giant, domed skylights of iron and glass; and the dignified appeal of the city's parks. Anyone who has been to Paris will recognize the Champs-Élysées with its broad, tree-lined avenue featuring the Arc de Triomphe de l'Étoile and the Place de la Concorde at its extremes in a direct line of vision; the Rue Royale, another straight-lined, dramatic roadway which begins at the Place de la Concorde and leads to the Church of the Madeleine at its terminus; and, of course, the Bois de Boulogne.

Napoléon III desired to make the Bois de Boulogne and the other parks within the city, areas which would give a special delight to the senses. Here in Philadelphia, these elegant Parisian *coups de grâce* are echoed in the graceful and dramatic Memorial Hall in Fairmount Park, which was the central building of the Centennial Exhibition in 1876, marking the hundredth anniversary of the Declaration of Independence; this was the first successful world's fair in the New World, and by far the most extensive. Memorial Hall, with its grand proportions, balustrades and statues, is domed by an iron and glass skylight which is so characteristically French that it cannot help but conjure up reveries of Paris. Similar in conceptual design to the

Memorial Hall (Fairmount Park)

Paris Opéra, the dome at night is lit up from its interior with a most pleasant green luminescence and can be seen from many vantage points along the Schuylkill River.

Fairmount Park is a phenomenon unto itself; the largest urban park in the world—almost 4,000 acres—the park evokes so much of the Belle Époque of the last half of the 19th century that it would be almost impossible to cover. The Belle Époque was an era of high collars, lace and parasols for the ladies, with elegant vested suits and high top hats for the gentlemen—as if plucked out of a work by Seurat or the Judy Garland movie *Meet Me in St. Louis*. The park contains beautiful brownstone portals leading to stairways along the banks of the Schuylkill, which are all the more romantic because

Fairmount Park delights

they go unused and are overgrown with vegetation, and Victorian gazebos with breathtaking views of the river. There is also a water-works for water purification, which was the first of its kind in the country, housed in a half-dozen small, classical structures at the foot of the Philadelphia Museum of Art to give testament to the grace and elegance of this bygone age.

*N*apoléon III's love of art was certainly not limited to the building arts. Every year he would visit the Salon, which was the official showplace of the newly created French art from the preceding year. In 1863, on his annual visit, he had been somewhat uninspired by the year's offerings and inquired as to what pieces had been refused by the selection committee. Among the rejected works was one that employed a new style of short brush-strokes by the artist Édouard Manet entitled *Déjeuner sur l'Herbe*. The new style was later to become known as "impressionism," and the Emperor was so taken with it that he ordered a new gallery to be created for its exhibition, the Salon des Réfusés—the "Gallery of Rejected Artists." The Belle Époque was the period which ushered in a flowering of the impressionist school and produced in France some of the most famous works and artists the world has come to know. Here in Philadelphia, a few blocks to the west of City Avenue and 54th Street, we have the honor of being home to the Barnes Foundation, which houses one of the finest collections of French impressionist and post-impressionist paintings in the world.

Albert Barnes (1872–1951) was one of those fabulously interesting Philadelphians who fall into the time-honored, community-service tradition of William Penn. Born into a working-class neighborhood of the city, he was brought up by a devout Methodist mother who took him to camp meetings and religious retreats when he was still a young boy. After graduating from Central High School, the prestigious, city-run institution which educated so many famous

Philadelphians, he took his M.D. degree from the University of Pennsylvania Medical School. With a special business acumen, he co-developed an antiseptic formulation called "Argyrol" and launched its manufacture in 1902, with facilities in Philadelphia, London and Australia. Needless to say, he became highly successful. His financial success was tempered, however, by a profound interest in the arts and a very real compassion for the working man. This was the era of Teddy Roosevelt, whose commitment to the environment and the working poor set the tone for national politics; while impressionist art, for its part, attempted to glorify the day-to-day life of the common man. In a similar vein, Dr. Barnes disliked inherited privilege and believed in the virtue of the ordinary man—much like our Founding Fathers 125 years before. He believed in the powerful human emotions which fine art could evoke in people, not just in its aesthetic appreciation, and he delighted in exposing his factory workers to his ongoing acquisition of contemporary fine art, right there in the factories. This was also the time that Sigmund Freud's writings were becoming recognized, and Dr. Barnes, as a physician, attempted to understand and to stimulate the minds of his factory employees through discussions about these fine works of art, as well as bettering their working conditions. In 1922, he created the Barnes Foundation, which took on a life of its own to serve as an instrument to make fine art accessible to everyone.

The Barnes Foundation boasts an extraordinary collection of masterpieces by Renoir (180), Cézanne (69) and Matisse (60), along with works by Picasso, Seurat, Rousseau, Modigliani, Soutine, Monet, Manet, Degas and many others. Together with the modern French collection in the Art Museum, this represents the largest, most significant group of impressionist and post-impressionist paintings outside Paris. A brochure from the Foundation quotes Ambroise Vollard, who said in 1936 that "a visit to the Barnes Foundation is in itself worth the trip to America."

In the era before the First World War, a grandiose plan similar to that devised by Georges Haussmann for Paris was drafted for Philadelphia in the creation of the Benjamin Franklin Parkway extending from City Hall to the Art Museum. It was designed by the French architect Jacques Gréber and represents an urban renewal effort which rivaled that of Haussmann in the creation of the Champs-Élysées in Paris. The Parkway has often been referred to as "*our* Champs-Élysées." Stately buildings taking their inspiration from their French counterparts and superb fountains that are as dramatic as they are beautiful, by day and by night, grace the broad, straight-lined thoroughfare from City Hall to the Art Museum. Buildings such as the Philadelphia Free Library and the Municipal Court, whose facades are modeled after the Ministry and the Hôtel de Crillon on the Place de la Concorde in Paris, were cast in the true French classic style, which succeeded the French Second Empire and Gothic Revival styles of the last half of the 19th century.

Two obelisks which flank the Parkway at midpoint, practically facing the Free Library and the Municipal Court buildings, display Civil War reliefs which are not unlike the dramatic and spiritually moving reliefs of the "Marseillaise" found upon the Arc de Triomphe de l'Étoile on the Champs-Élysées. Their central positioning with the Franklin Institute on one side, the Library and Municipal Court on the other, and within clear view of the magnificent Swann Fountain on Logan Circle in the middle of the Parkway—and, of course, the Art Museum in the distance—creates Philadelphia's "Place de la Concorde." I especially like to walk along the inner loop of the Parkway at night: the elegant fountains are beautifully lit with soft, blue-green reflections from their collecting pools and their oxidized metalwork, and the illuminated sprays of water give sweet contrast to the darkened sky; the landmark buildings are always in view to dramatize the Parkway's classic beauty, and it is relatively safe to walk in the company of joggers and other promenaders who are always in proximity in all kinds of weather, at every season of the year. This is the closest my senses can send me into an evening in Paris; the fact that there is less traffic and less commercialism here on the Parkway than on the Champs-Élysées makes the walk even more captivating.

At 22nd Street and the Parkway is a jewel of a building known as the Rodin Museum. Designed by one of the 20th century's most versatile architects, Paul Philippe Cret, the building is modeled on a château in France where Rodin had his studio. The Rodin Museum has the largest collection of sculptures by the late-19th-century sculptor to be found outside France and was commissioned by theater owner Jules Mastbaum in the 1920s. Cret also designed the Barnes Foundation building, Rittenhouse Square, the Federal Reserve Bank and the Benjamin Franklin Bridge, and he helped Jacques Gréber design the Parkway itself.

The Art Museum and so many other buildings in Philadelphia from the late 19th and early 20th centuries were directly influenced by the École des Beaux Arts, the School of Fine Arts, in Paris. The school's beginnings can be traced to 1795, when it replaced the Royal

Rodin on the Parkway

Inner courtyard of the Rodin Museum

Academy of Arts, the latter having a bad ring in the "revolutionary" ears of the citizens of Paris. Initially, the school taught the techniques of painting and about twenty-five years thereafter, architecture was added to the curriculum. All the great French artists and architects, and many others from around the world, came to Paris to take their training in what was considered the art and design center of the world. With the success of the impressionist painters of the late 19th century, whose styles and vision had become so highly individualized, the École began to lose its influence in painting, but its domination in the architectural arts became even greater. The "Beaux

Arts" style, as it is called, was one which employed classical architectural elements cast in the most monumental, dramatic presentations—from the Greco-Roman to the Romanesque and the Gothic along with a smattering of Egyptian and Byzantine motifs.

In Europe, every high school student is familiar with Romanesque and Gothic architecture. Their cultures are deeply reflected in these building styles which are so enmeshed in their countries' histories. Briefly, the Romanesque (or "Roman-like") style had its origins in the monasteries of 11th-century France. At a time when the Church found itself to be the only unifying force in medieval Europe, the Romanesque style developed uniform characteristics which made use of the rounded arch and basilica designs of ancient Rome along with heavy walls to support the structure; the walls doubled as fortifications in the politically unsettling times that extended into the early 13th century. As the Church needed to spread the Gospel among a populace which could neither read nor write, the capitals atop the rounded columns and the reliefs within the porticos of Romanesque churches were made as graphic as possible to depict Biblical scenes with which the people could identify. Romanesque architecture is rooted to the ground; to be alone in one of these hauntingly beautiful little sanctuaries—be it in Armenia, the Iberian peninsula or in the French countryside—is to eclipse a thousand years of history and to feel a personal communion with the Creator.

By contrast, the Gothic, which is the term applied to the new architectural style originating in 12th-century France, developed the pointed arch and a new engineering that shifted the building's support away from the walls and onto collateral points of stress by the use of flying buttresses and abutments. This freed up the walls from their supporting roles to give added focus to their dramatic, spiritual effects, allowing for the development of magnificent stained glass windows which sometimes covered almost the whole area of the wall. No longer earthbound like the Romanesque, the Gothic style soared to new heights as part of an attempt to foster a heightened spirituality among the people. This building style exemplified not only a new spiritual direction, but also manifested the wealth coming from the new commercialism which began to take hold in the latter medieval period. The great cathedrals were as much a source of local civic pride as they were temples of spirituality. Toward the end of the 15th century, Gothic architecture became even more ornate with filigree embellishments and delicate craftsmanship in which stonemasons began to produce complex designs that rivaled the intricate work of fine jewelry-makers. And nowhere does Gothic architecture attain such delicate beauty, such intricacies, as that seen in the French Gothic. It is so characteristic that once appreciated, it seems to jump out at you wherever it appears. We are fortunate to have superb examples of original French Romanesque and Gothic architectural elements from the medieval period in the Philadelphia Museum of Art, and throughout the city there are glorious reproductions of portals and windows in the French Gothic style.

The Beaux Arts style of the late 19th and early 20th centuries took these characteristic elements and greatly accentuated them to create an even greater dramatic effect with grandiose stone archway entrances and a plethora of superb ornamental ironwork to complement the arched settings. And just as the classical forms of antiquity gave rise to the Romanesque and, in turn, to the Gothic, 19th-century architecture recapitulated the sequence with a progression from the relatively unadorned classical styles of Napoléon in the first half of the century, to the Second Empire classicism of Napoléon III (1850–1875), which incorporated sculpture and more stylized French Renaissance motifs, to the revived Romanesque and Gothic styles of the last quarter of the century—all in the same, albeit abbreviated, sequence as that which occurred in history. The Beaux Arts style simply, and beautifully, magnified these styles to bring us into the modern age of 20th-century architecture. There are many structures in Philadelphia, both secular and ecclesiastical, which incorporate elements of the Romanesque and Gothic. With its dramatic oversizing of these forms, the Beaux Arts style gave them new life and a certain striking presence which had not been seen before.

On some conscious level, people often make mental comparisons between Philadelphia and New York—and New York, generally, seems to come out on top with Philadelphia's taking its place as some sort of historical backwater. But there are remarkable differences which must be kept in mind as to how these two great cities grew and how they faced the same challenges of trade and immigration, manufacturing and industrialization, and the great social changes which were to follow. Philadelphia, as has been seen, began with the highest American ideals of social equality and industriousness among her colonists. Even though other urban centers like New York and Boston predate the establishment of Philadelphia, it was because of the ever-present economic and social planning of community-minded citizens like William Penn, Benjamin Franklin and so many others that Philadelphia grew into the largest, wealthiest and most beautiful city in the country by the time of the Revolution and continued to grow well into the 19th century. Becoming the national capital from 1790 to 1800 underscored Philadelphia's importance among American cities and the attempts by the new towns springing up in the West to duplicate her organization and custom during the 18th century reinforced that importance. With the coming of the 19th century, however, while Philadelphia began to lose political influence to the new capital in Washington and while New York began to surpass her in population, the Quaker City's importance as a manufacturing and industrial center grew steadily as the century progressed.

The surrounding farmlands provided Philadelphia with a rich agricultural base to serve her urban population, but the city was also blessed with an ample supply of water power and rich deposits of coal and iron to set the stage for the coming industrialization. The power of steam, coal and oil fueled manufacturing and commerce so that the great Centennial Exhibition of 1876, which celebrated the hundredth anniversary of the signing of the Declaration of Independence, was as much a trade show of Philadelphia's progress into the new age of industrialization as it was a birthday party for the country. It was probably the most extensive and sensational world's fair the world had seen or would see for many years to come. The work force which manned the new factories was made up of skilled or semi-skilled laborers whose jobs passed from father to son or who came from the surrounding rural areas. In contrast to New York, which aggressively exploited the labor of the new immigrants arriving from foreign shores, Philadelphia tended to discourage immigration in the 19th century, probably to protect its semi-skilled work

Ceres, goddess of agriculture, awaits her turn

force from the influx of unskilled foreign laborers who were attracted to the city and its advantages. That is not to say that there were no great migrations of workers into the city; there were many, to be sure, but instead of the growing confrontations between labor and management arising from the extreme living and working conditions which were so dramatically seen in New York's tenements and sweat shops, Philadelphia's arrivals tended to assimilate into their new work and living environments, usually within the homes of extended family members.

In the same vein, the middle-class values of neighborhoods and home ownership remained as Philadelphia institutions. As Manhattan became exceedingly crowded and land values steadily increased, workers had to content themselves with "tenement" living conditions until they were able to afford to move out of the city into more comfortable housing. On the other hand, it was here in Philadelphia that the country's first row homes were built in the early 18th century, which helped to accommodate the growing numbers of new residents. And row homes carried little connotation of status; there were elegant row homes in the older sections of the city and more simply constructed row homes within view of the new factories going up within the city. Philadelphians prided themselves on owning their own homes and urban renewal projects generally met with a consensus by the people of the neighborhoods. With the great waves of immigration at the turn of the century, New York, on the other hand, was forced to grow even more vertically, into the sky, and with the great advances in engineering and steel building construction of the 20th century, some of the greatest marvels in the building arts—the skyscrapers—were erected on the isle of Manhattan during this period. But, again, with costlier land values and an ever-increasing population, home ownership was attained by only the very few—a legacy which continues today.

This urban renewal in Manhattan also bulldozed much of New York's early history. Philadelphia, on the other hand, had more room to grow, and the city's preservation societies, which had begun to form in the early 1800s, attempted to save many of the notable historical buildings from the onslaught of "commercial progress." Some of the buildings were even moved, brick by brick, to locations such as Fairmount Park. Philadelphia was therefore able to conserve much more of her historical past than other urban centers, and the fact that the city had such a great number of significant monuments to begin with means that today there is more visible American history here in Philadelphia than in practically all the other urban centers on the eastern seaboard combined. When John Kennedy became President in 1961, Mrs. Kennedy's first project was to redecorate the White House; she started in Philadelphia by going through the 18th-century houses of Fairmount Park to gather her ideas on authentic American decor.

In my walks around the city, I am always amazed at how many new discoveries I can make in a day's walk. Philadelphia is not one of those cities whose restored areas consist of five or six square blocks of exhibition buildings; her notable history is not contained in any one single section of town. There are significant buildings and streets from all eras of our history to be found throughout the city. From glorious civic monuments of the 18th and 19th centuries, to tiny, tree-lined streets, eight to ten feet wide, flanked by rows of two- and three-story period houses with little dormer windows and shutters, to houses and monuments showing French influence; from the austere and functional First Empire style to the modified classicism and embellishments of the Second Empire, which evoke the Belle Époque of the mid- to late 19th century, to a plethora of Romanesque and Gothic architectural elements in civic as well as ecclesiastical structures through the closing years of the century— Philadelphia gives life to them all. The Beaux Arts style, which became so popular at the beginning of the 20th century, reworked the Classical, Romanesque, Gothic, Egyptian and Byzantine styles to give a monumental quality to the special characteristics of each of

these styles. This not only heightened their dramatic effect, but also included new artistic expressions of ornamental ironwork, large areas of glass and elegant traceries in stone imparting an elegance heretofore unseen.

Philadelphia's European character developed largely in the late 19th and early 20th centuries and paralleled much of what was occurring in Paris and London during the same time. The great London Fire in the 1660s and the social upheavals in 18th-century Paris did much to level the general layouts of the two cities, leading to great efforts toward urban renewal in both places. During the 1800s, Philadelphia found itself in a similar state of development.

A typical 19th-century street in Center City

Elegant vista along the Schuylkill in late spring (Strawberry Mansion Bridge with Memorial Hall in the distance)

The great numbers of French émigrés who came to the city provided the nucleus for an interest in French design, an aesthetic which dominated European taste throughout much of the 19th century. The prosperity gained from industrialization and from the new sources of power that steam and coal afforded, along with closer cultural ties to Europe, paralleled the emergence of new building technologies and styles, with most of these innovations coming from Paris or from American architects trained at the École des Beaux Arts. The Centennial Exhibition of 1876 further accentuated the city as a focal point for these new architectural expressions. In addition to being a vital center for industrial expansion and trade, Philadelphia had become the showplace for much of the cultural refinement and sophistication of the 19th century, which made it even more open to the new building ideas.

During the First World War, Philadelphia gained the sobriquet of the "Arsenal of Democracy" for its prolific production of war matériel, and the celebration of the war's end seemed especially jubilant here. The prosperity of the 1920s further stimulated the great urban renewal project of the Benjamin Franklin Parkway with its magnificent buildings of Beaux Arts and French Classical styles. The Parkway was a tremendous achievement in the city's development and like Haussmann's creation of the Champs-Élysées fifty years before, it represented a special joy that was taken in the beautification of our city; it also reflected a reaffirmation of the city's future. Its French design and execution would evoke the glory and permanence of Philadelphia for future generations. The Parkway's completion created a link in the joining of Center City with Fairmount Park, having City Hall and the Art Museum at its opposite ends.

One of the most striking monuments along the Parkway is the magnificent Swann Fountain in the middle of Logan Circle. The fountain stands at the midpoint of the Parkway at Logan Circle, which had been one of the five original park squares laid out by William Penn more than 200 years before. It had become a circle on taking center stage as a rotary roadway in the construction of the Parkway; previously, it was known as Logan Square. The Swann Fountain was named in honor of William Carey Swann, a 19th-century physician who had founded the Philadelphia Fountain Society which worked to build drinking fountains for people and drinking troughs for horses throughout the city; these drinking troughs were generally in the form of elegant stone sculptures and are still to be seen in Fairmount Park and Center City.

Three recumbent figures, representing the three prime waterways of Philadelphia, are the fountain's theme. They lie like three spokes of a wheel projecting out into a circular pool of fanciful frogs and turtles which spout their sprays toward the three principal figures. The male figure dominates the trio in size and personality and represents the mighty Delaware River in the form of a Lenni Lenape Indian ("Lenni-Lenape" means "real men" in the local Indian tongue) from the earliest days of the colony. It is a graceful work which projects a very masculine strength, but without the slightest hint of arrogance. The figure faces the site on the Delaware where Penn was supposed to have made the original treaty with the Indians; he holds what appears to be a carp above his head from which the fountain spouts its watery spray. The adult female figure, on the other hand, is soft, demure and quintessentially feminine; she represents the Schuylkill River. She holds a swan above her head from which water flows forth; the swan may have been included as a pun on the doctor's name. The "Schuyler Kill," meaning "hidden river," begins in central Pennsylvania and flows gently toward its mouth at the Delaware below the present-day city limits. On the early explorations up the Delaware in the 1600s, the mouth of the river had initially been missed and, thereafter, it had become known as the "hidden river." The Schuylkill is a gentler, more nurturing waterway, abundant with fish and luxuriant with vegetation along its banks. The earliest European settlers of this area—the Swedes, the Finns and the Dutch—were often to be found along the idyllic banks of the Schuylkill. In fact, a little stone cottage with a gambrel roof

A Parisian setting for Logan Circle

and Dutch doors still sits upon a small hill overlooking the Schuylkill along the West River Drive; it supposedly dates from the 1660s, even before the arrival of William Penn himself. The female figure representing the Schuylkill, although gazing down in a most demure manner, directs herself to the site where the river empties into the Delaware.

The third figure represents the Wissahickon, a small river which empties into the Schuylkill just above the East Falls area. She is rep-

Swann Fountain, Logan Circle

resented as a young girl—a nymph, as it were—who emerges from a rich area of headland and woodland, which has largely been preserved within the Fairmount Park system, thanks to the forward-thinking preservationists of early-19th-century Philadelphia. She also holds a swan above her head and faces her *débouchement* into the Schuylkill above the Falls.

The sculptor of these striking figures was the second of a famous family of sculptors, Alexander Stirling Calder (1870–1945). His father, Alexander Milne Calder, was responsible for the statuary on City Hall, and Stirling Calder's son, Alexander Calder, acquired fame with a remarkable group of mobiles which hang in the atrium of the Art Museum. The artful genius of these three generations of sculpting Calders can be followed along the course of the Parkway itself. A. S. Calder was a native Philadelphian who had studied under Thomas Eakins at the Pennsylvania Academy of the Fine Arts and then, in Paris, at the École des Beaux Arts. These classic, monumental abstractions of our rivers are dignified and beautifully poetic, yet they convey in the most striking manner the qualities inherent within these three waterways, as described by the early inhabitants of the area, both the natives and the first Europeans.

The classic dignity projected from the Logan Circle sculptures has a very French quality which is not so dissimilar from the immutable, unremitting expression in the face of "Our Lady of the Harbor," the Statue of Liberty, or in Eugène Delacroix's *Liberty Leading the People*. But aside from the sculptures themselves, Logan Circle has its own particular, Parisian quality which imparts to the city wayfarer familiar with a Paris stroll that special feeling which is closely akin to finding oneself in the gardens of the Tuileries, perhaps. The walkways are of a special white, compacted sand like that seen in the parks of Paris and the benches, with narrow boards which conform more comfortably to the back, have a European look and feel that are unlike the majority of public benches that we Americans have become accustomed to. There is a small brick building with a pitched metal roof, blue-green in color from its exposure to the ele-

A MERCIFUL MAN
IS MERCIFUL TO HIS BEAST

One of several 19th-century combination drinking fountains which still dot Center City and the Park. The side for humans faces the sidewalk.

ments, which serves as the pump house for the fountain while at the same time bestowing some structural permanence to the small oasis. And all around are trees and flowers which are respectfully cared for by the public as well as by the gardeners. The marble, scrolled daybeds upon which our three waterway figures recline somehow remind me of the classic scrolls at Napoléon's tomb at the Hôtel des Invalides and the street lights are fittingly 19th-century; all in all, it gives me a sense of being transposed in time and place, so that even the frenetic pace of modern-day automobile traffic coursing around the fountain seems to fade into oblivion, once within the confines of this magic area which has become known as Logan Circle.

The 1920s and '30s gave testimony to the decade of prosperity and the Depression years in Philadelphia as they did throughout the rest of the country, but probably in a more exaggerated way here in the city because of our prodigious industries and resources. But once again, Philadelphia's production prowess surged with patriotic pride to support the war effort during the Second World War.

Postwar prosperity and the stimulation of more automobile production brought about a major population shift. The resulting suburban sprawl, with new housing developments at every turn, drained the cities of their tax-based incomes. Industries, likewise, were soon to follow suit in their exodus from higher taxes, aging factory facilities and the less skilled work force which remained in the inner cities. The relative peace and prosperity of the 1950s and early '60s fostered a frivolous age which brought new prominence to Philadelphia with television phenomena like Dick Clark's *American Bandstand* and *The Mike Douglas Show*. But like so many other American urban centers in the following decades of the 1960s and '70s, Philadelphia found itself a battleground in the resolution of the country's social problems. A strong, unified police force and the fact that Philadelphia had a proportionately greater number of homeowners probably spared it some of the devastation seen in other cities throughout these turbulent times. But in the late 1970s and into the '80s, the city once again began to prosper, with skyscraper construction, elegant restaurants and a special interest in restoring her historical monuments.

Food has had a fine tradition in Philadelphia. When the Continental Congress met here in 1774, and lodgings were provided by the many inns and boardinghouses, the delegates often found themselves overwhelmed by the bountiful and tasty morsels that were to be had. Many wrote home about how well they feasted while they were here, and this tradition of fine food found renewed expression in the vigor of Center City's redevelopment by way of a renaissance in restaurants of haute cuisine. Monsieur Georges Perrier, master chef of Le Bec-Fin, gained worldwide recognition with his five-star restaurant, followed by others featuring French and "fusion" cuisine. These new restaurants came together to create a culinary oasis within Philadelphia, and the 1990s witnessed a progression of offshoots from these original watering holes which formed another new circle of elegant restaurants rivaling the finest offerings to be had in international cuisine. Philadelphia had once again become a world-class destination for gastronomes.

Still, Philadelphia is very much an American city, which is why so many new towns springing up in the heartland modeled themselves after it; a visitor from Charleston or Boston could equally find himself at home here along her tree-lined streets of handsome red brick houses and among a generally gracious populace. She was conceived in the highest American ideals and this spirit, this American graciousness, spread throughout all segments of her population. Commercially, the city developed as a trading port to rival all the other ports along the eastern seaboard, and she developed lines of communication throughout the hinterland and extending to many trading centers on foreign shores. Politically, Philadelphia served as the gathering place for the country's representatives during the formative years when the thirteen colonies were struggling to transform themselves into the United States of America. In the first ten years of nationhood, when the city served as the national capital, there was a feeling among Philadelphians, and many others in the rest of the country, that here was a city, dignified and beautiful, to which all Americans could look with pride as the capital of their new country.

Yet the city developed a maturity and sophistication that went well beyond her quintessential American character to rival the elegance of the European capitals as well. Philadelphia had been at the forefront of the Industrial Revolution during the 19th century and with her vast natural resources and the amassing of capital from this industrialization, the city's focus on building and design had become more international—and the international influences, especially during the 19th century, had largely been dictated from Paris. This was true for the rest of Europe, as well. But it was for this reason that our Hôtel de Ville—City Hall—was cast in the French Renaissance

The magnificent Bellevue Hotel

style of the Second Empire; that our most beautiful hotel, the Bellevue, is a Beaux Arts classic; that Memorial Hall in Fairmount Park is reminiscent of Parisian monuments of the Belle Époque which are so strikingly beautiful, both by day and by night; that the Benjamin Franklin Parkway, which adds such grace to the city's form, is a replica of Haussmann's creation of the Champs-Élysées some seventy years earlier. The monuments which line her course are so French in appearance that for someone fortunate enough to be familiar with Paris, it is as if some transoceanic double-take were at work here.

Add to this the many restaurants offering haute cuisine from the proto-renaissance of about twenty-five years ago, together with those of the newer wave which is still in progress, along with delightful sidewalk cafés and elegant boutiques that could just as well be found upon the Left Bank and coffeehouses whose French roast warms your sense of smell as no other aroma can. Add to this the wealth of French impressionist and post-impressionist masterpieces at the Barnes Foundation and the Art Museum, exceeded in sheer numbers only by Paris, as well as the Rodin Museum with more of the sculptor's work than any other place outside France. Consider a new high-rise French hotel in Center City within a district recently designated as the new "French Quarter"—all these things point to a city which harbors more than its American historical monuments.

Philadelphia is, indeed, a treasure that more and more people are beginning to discover. She is a visual encyclopedia of our historical past like no other American city that fortune and good will have preserved for the present generations. Her buildings and parks, her thoroughfares and monuments, all attest to our accomplishments in coming together as a people to bring about a new social organization through the wisdom of the Enlightenment and the words of the Founding Fathers. They attest, as well, to the greatness of the French contribution to our city, not only in the ideals of the Enlightenment of 18th-century France and the strength of French support in the fight for liberty, but also in the inspiration of French art and architecture throughout the 19th and 20th centuries. As such, Philadelphia has so much to offer the visitor and as a public trust, we have the obligation to preserve and protect her, as our forebears did in the past, so that she will retain that special individuality which reflects upon our own individuality as Americans.

French country living in the Mt. Airy
section of the city

1 French Country Living

*I*n the northwestern section of the city lie the suburbs of Mount Airy, Chestnut Hill and Germantown. Germantown has deep roots—Quaker roots—which go back to the 1680s, and was an independent town of historical significance long before it became incorporated into the city of Philadelphia in the mid-19th century. A drive along Germantown Avenue from Broad Street offers a kaleidoscope of American history from all periods, including scattered areas of modern-day commercialism and dilapidation, but with patience, the wayfarer is led back into the 18th century. President Washington's residence was the Deshler-Morris House, at 5267 Germantown Avenue, during the summer and fall of 1793, when the yellow fever epidemic was taking its toll throughout the city. Not only did he summon Jefferson, Hamilton and the rest of his cabinet to the house for their official meetings, but he and Martha also lived there and grew very fond of the place. It was the temporary "White House" until he could return to the Executive Mansion on High (Market) Street, between 5th and 6th Streets. In 1777, the famous Battle of Germantown was fought on the steps and grounds of Cliveden, at 6401 Germantown Avenue. This was the battle which caused the French to take a more serious view of the Americans' fight for independence.

A staunch little community of Dutch Quakers and Mennonites

in the beginning, with an overlay of German pietists around 1700, Germantown was an idyllic, single-street village, surrounded by orchards and grounded in the linen-weaving trade. These Germantown Friends (Quakers) were of a different "cloth" from their nearby brethren, the English Quakers in Philadelphia. In the late 1680s, the Germantown Friends were the first to denounce slavery with public outcries, only to be rebuffed by the English Quakers of the city, who felt this issue was too "complicated" to deal with. Yes, Germantown in its early days was a community unto itself, producing fine linen and high-minded, independent townsmen.

In the 1870s, while the railroad was extending itself westward along the old Lancaster Road to foster the creation of the elegant Main Line suburb west of the city, Henry Howard Houston, an executive of the Pennsylvania Railroad, conceived the idea of developing an upper-class suburb just north of Germantown on about 3,000 acres of farmland. It had already been incorporated into the city of Philadelphia and was bounded on the western edge by the beautiful headlands and woodlands of Fairmount Park, which in turn bordered the Schuylkill. Houston called the community "Wissahickon Heights" because of its setting with the Wissahickon River running through it, and intended his community to be an elegant, reclusive enclave of the Episcopalian (Anglican) elite. This marked the beginning of the Chestnut Hill and Mount Airy areas of the city. It is ironic that the Germantown Quakers and the Chestnut Hill and Mount Airy Episcopalians should be neighbors; after all, 150 years before, the Quakers had been under such oppression from the Anglicans in the mother country that they came to "Penn's Woods" to make a new start to their lives, only to find themselves once again juxtaposed, but seemingly more at peace, with each other in this bountiful, new land of America. In order to carry out his grand scheme of urban development, Houston persuaded the railroad to build a special branch into this northwestern section of the city, which would later become known as Chestnut Hill.

Medieval musings (Mt. Airy)

Houston's idea was to build distinctive houses for the well-to-do which would stand out from other suburban developments of "look-alike" houses. From these beginnings, he set the stage for the creation of something quite unique. Chestnut Hill and Mount Airy have some of the most romantic, most dignified and most fabled houses I have ever seen in America. Without exaggeration, rambling through the streets and roadways of these two sections of the city takes me into another period in time—childhood fantasies of faraway places take on a degree of substance here; the 19th century seems to come alive as I have never seen it elsewhere. Every "old manse" out of the "Hardy Boys" or "Nancy Drew" comes back to life as I had pictured them in my mind as a young adolescent. I can remember how awestruck I was as a kid on seeing the mansions of Palm Beach, but in truth, I cannot remember any one area with so many glorious houses as these two sections of Philadelphia, Chestnut Hill and Mt. Airy. Even the Main Line with all its elegance and "old money" pales in comparison, at least to me. As in Center City, the wayfarer could wander for days or months and still be struck with a glorious new "find" within these two enclaves.

When Henry Houston died in 1895, his son-in-law, Dr. George Woodward, took over Chestnut Hill's development. During the "Roaring 20s," Woodward engaged the architectural services of Robert McGoodwin, who had studied at the École des Beaux Arts, to create a group of Norman-French houses because Dr. Woodward had become so taken with the houses of the small towns and villages of Normandy when he toured this province of northwestern France. Sometimes referred to as the French Village, these houses are as

French Village (Mt. Airy)

stunning as they are distinctive. I have never seen anything quite like them on this side of the Atlantic, except, of course, in the Canadian province of Québec. And even in Québec, they seem to lack the setting or feeling of composition that the French Village possesses. High-pitched, slate roofs with overhanging eaves that curve outward; swooping gables with high, thick chimneys and walls of the local fieldstone or schist (the local metamorphic stone which can easily be split in parallel planes, hence the term "schist") and lots of turrets with their cone-shaped toppings make the French Village a vision unto itself. What strikes me as distinctively French, however, are the well-proportioned dormer windows and their fancy, stone-scrolling encasements which abound from the high-pitched roofs, and the narrow, vertical apertures in the turrets, which are really vestiges from the times when they served for defense. The Normans, or Norsemen, were Vikings who aggressively overran the coastal regions of much of Europe during the early Middle Ages, but instead of simply "raping and pillaging," as so frequently happened during those unsettling times, the Norsemen took to these lands and became the dominant force. They even gave their name to this region of northwestern France—Normandy. The houses are solid and substantial; they could easily be conceived as small fortresses which would faithfully protect their inhabitants from intrusion, and literally give meaning to the old phrase that a man's house is his castle.

Lost in the French countryside (Mt. Airy)

Moving deeper into Chestnut Hill, another collection of French architectural delights centers upon Hampton Road at Crefeld Avenue in the northernmost reaches of this section. The house known as High Hollow, designed by the architect George Howe for himself while a student at Beaux Arts, is a glorious dwelling which conjures up the image of a château in the French countryside. Nestled within a ravine along a gentle slope, the house has even grander and higher perspectives than those of the French Village, yet it blends harmoniously into its setting. Again, we find the use of the local schist (fieldstone) and brick for the walls, but now there are accents of red-brick stringcourses which seem to add distinction,

A solid Norman manse (Mt. Airy)

while at the same time helping the house to blend further into its background of stately trees and shrubs. But the *coup de grâce* is, without question, the glorious, thimble-topped turret that stands at the corner nearest the entrance. This Beaux Arts rendition of the thimble-topped turret is a more graceful expression of the classic, cone-shaped top and can also be seen at Chantilly, a château which was being rebuilt in the 1880s, north of Paris. Howe must have seen the château of Chantilly only a dozen or so years after its completion when he was in residence at Beaux Arts; for like High Hollow, here, too, at Chantilly are stringcourse accents and thimble-topped turrets to add distinction to the structure. But to be more accurate in terms of architectural appearance, these thimble-topped turrets were Beaux Arts expressions of the earliest period of the Renaissance in which this shape of the tower usually flanked the toll-house gates along the major roadways of late-15th- and early-16th-century France. The outbuildings at High Hollow have similar stringcourse accents and there is an arcade, seen from the rear of the house, which allows a level approach to the pool from the main house, so as to break the angle of the slope of the ravine. I have never seen houses like these in our country. They can figuratively transport the wayfarer back to the French countryside of earlier times, or to our own romantic reveries of the past.

High Hollow (Chestnut Hill)

Fairmount Park

2 Fairmount Park

Fairmount Park is the largest urban park in the country with almost 4,000 acres of land. It bestrides both banks of the Schuylkill north of Center City and continues up the Wissahickon Valley for several miles before entering Montgomery County. It also includes the Benjamin Franklin Parkway, which is considered its link to Center City. The park's borders are so irregular that even native Philadelphians living within its surroundings can be hard-pressed to say where the park begins or ends in so many places; it is a vast, amorphous area with a natural beauty that, to me, is without parallel. But how could it not be? Here are acres and acres of land preserved with two of our principal waterways in their midst. And public use and enjoyment of these lands are shared by the great majority of Philadelphians—rich and poor, black and white, young and old. Originally preserved for protection of the city's water supply from the Schuylkill's feeding into the waterworks at the foot of the bluff, which William Penn originally referred to as "Faire Mount," the park grew to its present size after years of city consolidation and public donation. Today, the Philadelphia Museum of Art sits directly on top of "Faire Mount."

Aside from protecting the water supply, there was also a popular movement in the 1850s for naturally landscaped areas to be set aside for public use as parks, just as Central Park in Manhattan had

Solitude on the Schuylkill

loomed in the minds of many New Yorkers, and President Millard Fillmore had recommended the beautification of the public grounds in Washington, which later coalesced to form the Mall. The Lemon Hill estate, above the waterworks, that once belonged to Robert Morris had been owned by the city since 1844, but it came under direct city management through a city council ordinance in 1855, and it was held as a public trust and an addition to what was taking more definitive form as Fairmount Park. The reader may recall that this was also the time that Napoléon III was taking his initiatives to beautify the Bois de Boulogne and other city parks in Paris. Unfortunately, the Civil War years had tabled much of any progress here until the Fairmount Park Commission was appointed in 1867, two years after the war.

Fairmount Park has so many glorious things within its boundaries, both natural and man-made; the views along the Schuylkill are breathtaking in themselves with their undisturbed, natural vegetation and the gently flowing river running through the heart of the city. But when accented by elegant vestiges of the last half of the 19th century—the Belle Époque—there is beauty that even rivals that of the French capital with the Seine flowing through her heart. For instance, the view from the Strawberry Mansion Bridge, looking east, with Memorial Hall in the background, the old CSX railroad bridge slightly to the fore across the river and the tiny, tree-laden Peters Island, even more to the fore, being circumnavigated by the

The Waterworks and Boathouse Row

crew teams on the water is a sight which could never be duplicated, and one which would not be seen elsewhere in our great land. It is "old-world" elegant and thoroughly peaceful. The railroad bridge could have been built by the Romans 2,000 years ago with its rounded arches and water-worn abutments. And when I look at Memorial Hall, I can very easily forget about modern-day, 20th-century life and recall the grace and elegance of a bygone era, an era that took extreme pride in the beauty as well as the function of its buildings. In the same vein, the Strawberry Mansion Bridge itself, with its iron latticework and its graceful piers, and the Falls Bridge, slightly upstream, with its metal lattice, now in the form of a box to incorporate the roadway, possess delicate traceries in their guardrails which bow outwardly with quintessential grace from the borders of the roadway and are both dramatic and reminiscent of French fineries and attention to detail. Both these bridges have elegant and refined personalities which are distinctly 19th-century.

A little further upstream from the Falls Bridge lies the mouth of the Wissahickon River emptying into the Schuylkill. The Wissahickon forms one of the most striking visual effects as seen from any urban roadway in the country. An Alpine gorge cut out of headland and woodland greets the sojourner up the Lincoln Drive with an incomparable view of nature which has been preserved since the days of our city's founding.

But, to me, the crowning glory of Fairmount Park resides in the elegant edifice known as Memorial Hall and the Centennial Exhibition of 1876, for which the Hall was built and which marked the celebration of the country's 100th birthday.

As early as 1866, the idea of a centennial exposition to be held in Philadelphia had been voiced by supporters from several parts of the country, and it continued to gather momentum over the following three years, despite the misgivings of many others. The doubters feared that if there were to be an international exposition, there would remain the question of whether other nations would partici-

Our "Pont du Gard" (Manayunk)

pate. New York had attempted an Exhibition of the Industry of All Nations in 1853–54, but it had been a commercial venture in which there had been little involvement from abroad, and it had not been considered successful. Secondly, could American industry and arts compete so as to be seen in a favorable light among the other nations of the world? And, thirdly, could the country afford a world's fair? The international exhibitions that had taken place in Europe had increasingly required strong financial backing from their respective governments, and our national treasury after the Civil War and Reconstruction was not in a healthy state. Where would the money come from? Aside from these very real hurdles, as the exposition idea gathered momentum, Boston, New York and Washington would also compete for the venue. But it was Philadelphia which won the day as the chosen site, mainly because of the constant efforts on the part of local leaders of business and industry together with the strong support of city and state legislators.

The idea to celebrate the 100th anniversary of the signing of the Declaration of Independence came at an auspicious time; the bitterness from the years of the Civil War and Reconstruction had left the country spiritually divided, and an opportunity to begin the healing was here at hand in the proposed Centennial Exhibition. Philadelphia was a natural choice for several reasons. Firstly, here was the place where it all began; to celebrate the grand occasion among historical sites such as Independence Hall and Carpenters' Hall was to transcend the divisiveness of the recent years of civil strife and to remember a time when we Americans had been more cohesive and hopeful as a people. William Penn's "towne on the Delaware" had been a model of peace, prosperity and order, and its remarkable growth and ascent to preeminence as the nation's first capital went a long way toward moderating the strong feelings from the different sectors of the country. Secondly, along with the beauty of tradition, Philadelphia had developed a vibrant economy from her rapidly expanding industrialism, and the city had the agricultural resources to support a great influx of visitors. And, thirdly, the agricultural abundance seemed to mirror something of the graciousness of Philadelphians themselves—a visitor from Savannah could feel just as much at home here as a visitor from New York. It was as if the city represented a kind of matriarchal figure who would bring her children together again after so many years of civil strife.

But making the Centennial a reality required a great deal of effort and resources from the business and industrial leaders of the area, as well as the state and city legislators and the local newspaper columnists. Although Congress finally approved a bill creating the United States Centennial Commission in 1872, it was with the strict proviso that the federal government would not be liable for any of the expenses. With this in mind, a Centennial Board of Finance was created and authorized to sell up to $10 million in stock, in denominations of $10 a share, to cover the major expenses of the exposition. The city of Philadelphia contributed $1.5 million and the Commonwealth of Pennsylvania contributed $1 million. Congress *appropriated* $1.5 million in February 1876, three months before the opening of the fair, and after its closing in November, demanded the return of the full appropriation from the stockholders. Not only was this tight-fisted policy of Congress applied to the actual construction of the Exhibition, but to its promotion abroad, as well. A journalist, John Forney, consented to head a commission to visit Europe in 1874, and to personally invite the European nations to participate in the great event; he paid for it out of his own pocket. Of course, there had been a driving force to showcase the rapidly expanding industrialism of the city and its surroundings and to share in the technology of the day from other industrial countries; but once again, it was this magnificent volunteerism in the tradition of our founder, William Penn, which brought the vision of the Exhibition to reality.

Memorial Hall was intended as a permanent building before which stood three great, temporary structures that were the chief attractions: the Main Building, Machinery Hall and Agricultural Hall. The construction of the Main Building began in 1874. It was the largest building in the world at that time; it covered more than twenty-one acres and extended a full third of a mile along the front concourse. It consisted of an iron-lattice framework which rested on 672 stone piers with plenty of glass between the frames to take advantage of the natural lighting. Its central avenue was 120 feet wide and 1,832 feet long, the longest avenue of that width ever introduced into an exhibition building. Machinery Hall, alongside the Main Building, had a similar design but covered about fourteen acres. Next to Machinery Hall was Agricultural Hall, which was a huge structure of Gothic design with an iron and wood framework.

Memorial Hall, the central showcase, was designed by Hermann

Memorial Hall "de nuit"

Schwarzmann, a German-born engineer with the Fairmount Park
Commission, who traveled to Vienna to gather his ideas. Keep in
mind that French was still the *lingua franca* throughout Europe, and
Paris continued to be the art and design capital of the world; so, no
matter where Mr. Schwarzmann traveled, the French influence, especially that of the Second Empire, was the prevailing style. He chose a
design which was not so dissimilar in concept from that of the Paris
Opéra by Charles Garnier, which was begun in 1862 and not completed until 1875. The Paris Opéra, with its classical base together
with an admixture of Baroque and its glass and iron dome, is considered the most opulent expression of the Second Empire style in
France. Likewise, Memorial Hall, with its classical base, iron and

glass dome and plethora of statuary and balustrades, also brings to mind the architectural richness of the Second Empire style. It is a striking, elegant building which stands alone and sings *a cappella* of this architectural period from its vantage point overlooking the Schuylkill. I never tire of looking at it; from different angles and in different weather conditions, it always seems to take on new visions of beauty for me. In this sense, it is unique and a true classic in every sense of the word. The two bronze statues of Pegasus which flank the entrance to the Hall were once atop the Vienna Opera, but the Viennese felt that they were out of proportion with their structure, so they were subsequently procured by Philadelphian Robert Gratz for Memorial Hall's entranceway, where they seem to fit in very well. In some of the architectural guide books to the city, Memorial Hall is dubbed an example of the Beaux Arts style; this, to me, is a play on words which somehow misses the mark. L'École des Beaux Arts, the School of Fine Arts in Paris, was certainly the arbiter of architectural design of the age, but in the 1870s, the style in vogue and the one which predominated was that of the Second Empire. The mansard roof was not the *sine qua non* to delineate this style, as seen through the description of the Paris Opéra itself, which is generally taken as the pinnacle of Second Empire. The glass dome was first seen in 18th-century France, by the way, where glass and wood were used instead of the glass and iron of the Second Empire. But the elements of classical design found in Memorial Hall, together with its characteristic dome and rich adornment of statuary and balustrades, easily place it within this glorious period of the Second Empire. Memorial Hall and City Hall, our Hôtel de Ville, are the two finest examples of Second Empire architecture we have here in Philadelphia and they are both magnificent.

There were more than 200 buildings within the Exhibition grounds by opening day, including a house from most states of the Union and a Women's Pavilion of grand proportion, and they were all surrounded by a fence about three miles long. President Grant and members of Congress came to Philadelphia in December 1875 to get a sneak preview of how everything was progressing and they must have been suitably impressed, especially by the Main Building and Machinery Hall, which were nearly completed, for it was little more than a month thereafter that Congress was finally animated into voting to appropriate the $1.5 million loan to help defray the expenses. Out-of-town and foreign journalists, too, began to take note of this "phenomenon" which was beginning to unfold in Philadelphia.

The original plan had been to open in April 1876 to commemorate the anniversary of Lexington and Concord, but construction delays and last-minute confusion pushed the opening day back to May 10. By this date, frenzied anticipation had given way to a reality which was the product of a great deal of hard work by a great many people.

The opening day was fair and warm after an early-morning rain and the bell at Independence Hall rang to signal the moment, followed by all the bells in the city. The *New York Herald* reported that the opening-day crowd was the "largest ever assembled on the North

The Corliss engine in the center of Machinery Hall, Centennial Exhibition (Fairmount Park).
Courtesy of The Free Library of Philadelphia, Print and Picture Collection

American continent." The official count was placed at 186,272; for modern exhibitions to equal the impact of this figure, it would be necessary for 800,000 people to be present. The Emperor and Empress of Brazil together with President and Mrs. Grant officiated at the opening ceremonies and at the end of some flowery speeches, which must have been difficult for the throngs to hear, the two men grasped the valves that started the immense Corliss engine in Machinery Hall. This engine, which was probably the greatest wonder of the Exhibition, supplied the power via cogs and underground shafts to drive some 800 other machines at the fair. Everything seemed to be set into motion at once in an atmosphere of great anticipation. Although attendance figures fell during the next couple of months, owing in part to the sweltering weather conditions, toward the fall and the break in the weather, attendance exceeded all expectations and by the close of the fair in November, more than 10 million visitors had passed through the admission gates.

Philadelphia rose to the occasion as host to the country and the world. Food and lodgings were plentiful and relatively inexpensive; transportation was made available to the great masses making their way to the Exhibition grounds, and there was plenty of fresh water and no health epidemics throughout the course of the event. In terms of transportation, it was the railroads which really outdid themselves in making a success of the whole venture. For all the hoopla of the earlier European fairs, the aspect of mass transportation was not a part of their plans. The Pennsylvania Railroad and the Philadelphia and Reading Railroads, however, built special lines from the heart of the city right up to the main entrance, where there were three platforms and a circular turnabout. There were even special excursion trains from New York, Baltimore and Pittsburgh, and all the railroads lowered their rates to Philadelphia. Owing to these lower fares and the justification that the event was educational, as well as fun and exciting, the Philadelphia Centennial Exhibition became the country's first mass tourist mecca. Up to this point, it was only the rich who were accustomed to taking long vacation trips, but now Americans of all means were able to make the trip from every part of the nation. As a result, this great coming together to celebrate our country's accomplishments went a long way toward healing the wounds and moderating the bitterness of the past decades and re-forged a unified, national mentality to these United States of America. And it was to the credit of the business, industrial and civic leaders of Philadelphia that this great effort became a successful reality.

Although the Corliss engine was the big attention-grabber at the fair, not far behind were the new inventions of the telephone by Alexander Graham Bell ("My God, it talks!" exclaimed the Brazilian emperor); the Quadruplex Telegraph by Thomas Alva Edison, which was able to transmit several messages simultaneously; the air brake by George Westinghouse and the Pullman Palace Car by George Pullman. There were three electric arc lights which pushed back the darkness of night with a glowing brilliance, together with the enchanting, greenish luminescence coming from the gas-lit dome of Memorial Hall. The machine tools required to produce the new machines especially impressed the British and the Germans from the standpoint of quality and efficiency—so much so that these two powers strove to emulate American technological efficiency from this time forward. Yes, the Centennial Exhibition of 1876 proved to be a watershed that changed the course of history in many ways.

Fifty nations exhibited at the Exhibition and much of the fascination was centered on the two prefabricated buildings contributed by Japan. The Japanese had used common ceramic and cloth materials to create veritable *objets d'art*. Their prefab buildings also commanded a new respect with their graceful roof lines and porches, together with their rich ornamental carving and precision tilework. One of the leading architects of the day proclaimed that these Japanese structures were a "capital and most improving study to the careless and slipshod joiners of the Western world."

But perhaps the most visually dramatic sight at the fair was the

The mutual passion for liberty between the French and the American people, expressed visually through the Statue of Liberty. Courtesy of The Free Library of Philadelphia, Print and Picture Collection

arm and torch of the future Statue of Liberty, which was on display in a small, tented pavilion. This surreal representation propagated the idea of liberty as much as Delacroix's portrayal of Lady Liberty leading the French people to victory over tyrannical forces. The Statue of Our Lady of the Harbor, as most Americans know, was a gift from the French Republic to the people of the United States. The two nations seemed to remain linked as kindred spirits in their mutual love of liberty.

To native Philadelphians, the six months of the Centennial Exhibition proved to be a very heady time and provided the city's inhabitants with a new sense of confidence in the city's greatness and potential. It must have been a source of great pride for many Philadelphians to read in the *Chicago Tribune* of May 1, 1876, that staid old Philadelphia was gone, and that the city was "as cosmopolitan as Paris and as lively as Chicago."

To the tune of "Chim-chimeree"

3 Chim-chimeree

Chim-chimeree, chim-chimeree, chim-chimchiree,
A life of a chimney sweep, that is for me.
Chim-chimeree, chim-chimeree, chim-chimchiroo,
Good luck will rub off, when I shake hands with you,
And throw me a kiss and that's lucky, too.

The euphonious phrase "Deux Cheminées," the name of a fine, old French restaurant on Locust Street, works just as well, and is just as hard to dispel, as that childhood ditty from Walt Disney's *Mary Poppins.* "Deux Cheminées" means "two chimneys" in French, and, to me, flows as euphoniously as Disney's lyric. Follow me, if you will, through a few more free associations—*aux folies*—of a French connection within the City of Brotherly Love.

There are touches, nuances, everywhere which remind me of the French capital: the lampposts throughout Center City are quaintly European, or at least 19th-century; each dark green post is topped by an inverted beehive globe with tuning-fork metal joinings attaching it to its "old world" crown, complete with finial top, and when they appear in multiples, they seem to possess a distinctive French flavor. It was none other than our own patriarch of practicality, Ben

*Placid reflections of an elegant past—
Strawberry Mansion Bridge with
Memorial Hall in the distance*

Franklin, who suggested the multi-pane globe in the 18th century so
that if part of the lamp broke, only a part of the glass would have to
be replaced instead of the whole globe. This was the characteristic
lamppost of "Olde Philadelphia," and it certainly has its charm, as
well; the quaint little sets of windows, often seen as a trinity, retain a
special European look of grace. The banner proclaiming "Historic
Philadelphia," hanging from the modern-day lampposts within the
proximity of Independence Hall and the most tourist-trodden areas
of "Olde City," has as its background none other than the tricolor of
la douce France. Many of the subway stairs in Center City are covered
by a greenish-tinged glass canopy which is certainly not seen in the
New York subways, but has a certain kinship to the old glass Métro
coverings in Paris.

When I look into the heart of Center City to see our City Hall, 1420 Chestnut and the magnificent Bellevue Hotel, within three blocks of one another, I see Paris. When I pass along Walnut Street with its restaurants of well-known acclaim bearing French names, I see Paris. Residential buildings with names like the Versailles and the Touraine, within a few blocks south of Walnut, along with the famed Curtis Institute of Music, a Beaux Arts classic on Locust, make me think of Paris. When I come upon the Academy of Music, designed by Napoléon LeBrun in the 1850s, at Broad and Locust, and think of its gorgeous interior, I can almost visualize Monsieur le Fantôme swinging from the chandelier above a sea of red velvet or rising up from some false bit of flooring at a crashing, symphonic coda. In reality, the exterior of the Academy exists only in its original shell of brick; it was later to be covered with a classic facade which was to resemble La Scala in Milan, but with the approaching Civil War, the conservative exterior remained as it was.

Edgar Allan Poe, who had never been to Paris, wrote his famous "Murders in the Rue Morgue" in the early 1840s, while living at Seventh and Spring Garden Streets. He was inspired to write a work with a great deal of Parisian background and color while living in Philadelphia. Whence came his inspiration? Apropos, his Gothic tales of horror were much more appreciated by the French than by his American contemporaries.

The traceries of metal latticework from our 19th-century bridges over the Schuylkill, the Falls Bridge and the Strawberry Mansion Bridge, seem to hold a sense of déjà vu for me. The latter, with its high-rising arches and graceful piers, seen from the banks or from the water, presents a view reminiscent of that seen from under the Eiffel Tower on the banks of the Seine, especially when Memorial Hall sits royally in the background. The CSX railroad bridge might even rival the Pont Neuf from a distance. And, at night, the soft greenish luminescence emanating from the Hall's beautiful dome of iron and glass is *extraordinaire.*

And then there is the Parkway. From our City Hall, with its Second Empire–Renaissance design and its plethora of classic statuary by Alexander Milne Calder, to the grandeur of our Art Museum atop Faire Mount in its glorious Beaux Arts style, the Benjamin Franklin Parkway is purely French in concept and design. Ben himself would probably have been in awe of this magnificent roadway named in his honor. The fountains and the buildings are part of a unique setting and an exquisite architectural achievement, and I am taken with their beauty whenever I find myself on one of its roadways or walkways.

A Parkway perspective

Classical elegance of Logan Circle

The Swann Fountain, in the middle of Logan Circle, stands at the midpoint of the Parkway between City Hall and the Art Museum. When I am lucky enough to have the leisure to wander through the city and to come upon this oasis, it feels like the *coup de grâce* of all my Parisian reveries. This little plot of ground, together with the Parkway and the elegant buildings which flank it, is quintessentially Parisian and even succeeds in muting the frenetic sounds of the automobile traffic coursing around it.

From the heart of Center City, through the Parkway, to the banks of the Schuylkill with its resplendent vistas, this is a magnificent city which rivals the beauty and elegance of the "City of Lights" herself. *Avec un parfum de France partout.*

"L'élégance, tout simplement"

4 French Restaurants

As mentioned in the Introduction, food has had a fine tradition in Philadelphia. The delegates to the Continental Congress were generally awed at the bounty and the savory morsels which were to be had in the many inns and boardinghouses throughout the city.

During the Civil War, two volunteer organizations, the Union Volunteer Refreshment Saloon and the Cooper Shop Refreshment Saloon, took it upon themselves to feed the troop trains passing through the city from points north on their journeys south to the fronts. One soldier wrote, "As soon as we reached the city, we marched to the dining saloon . . . we entered the wash-room, a room large enough to accommodate sixty or seventy men to wash at a time. Then we were marched into a splendid hall, with room enough to feed 500 men at a time. There were gentlemen to wait on us, and they would come around and ask if we had plenty and urge us to eat more."

In the 19th century, fine French *pensions de famille* (boarding houses) could be found in the city. One of the most famous, and possibly the last of its kind, was the *pension* of Monsieur and Madame Allard on Walnut Street between 33rd and 34th Streets. It catered to the university crowd and served as a nucleus for the diffusion of French language, culture and, of course, cuisine. For those of us who have had the good fortune to travel in Europe, especially in the days of *Europe on $5 a Day*, the warmth and conviviality that some of these *pensions* accorded can easily be imagined.

It would appear that the seed of fine French cuisine had been latent from the beginnings of our fair city and had been fostered by Philadelphia's close connections with France since the time of the Revolution. Proportionately, we have more French "watering holes" than any other city in the U.S. This was the impetus for the city to designate a three-to-four-block area as the new French quarter, complete with a new, French high-rise hotel—Sofitel. But the real push behind the establishment of haute cuisine in recent times came from an enterprising chef by the name of Georges Perrier, owner of Le Bec-Fin on Walnut Street. *Condé Nast Traveler* has repeatedly named Le Bec-Fin ("The Fine Palate") as the best restaurant in America.

Monsieur Perrier has recently come out with a book of recipes from his famous establishment, and in the introduction he relates the story of learning his craft, *son métier,* and his coming to Philadelphia. Georges comes from a town in the province of Lyon, near the Swiss border, where gastronomy is especially apprized as part of the culture. He warmly recounts how his mother made the family *repas* the centerpiece for the family's togetherness and how every detail was attended to. The five children, Georges and his four siblings, would pick the fresh herbs and vegetables from the garden for the Sunday afternoon dinner, which was always the most specially prepared-for occasion, and she would show them how the freshest seasonings would enhance the definitive flavor of each dish. His father would carefully select the wine—based upon the menu, of course—and mealtimes became a very positive and significant part of Georges's life. His father was fastidious in his tastes and would say that this needed a little more of that and that that needed a little more of this. And young Georges began to demand more from himself, as his father seemed to demand more from him. But it was his mother, as he relates, who created the warmth that came *avec ces*

French restaurants

repas, and, in a way, the name of his famous restaurant probably stems from her careful nurturing of Georges's palate, *son bec fin*. When the time came to choose a career direction, Georges knew that the culinary arts were to be his choice. His father was a jeweler and his mother a physician, and both had wanted him to follow in their careers. In France, attaining the superlative is often linked to following a family tradition, and becoming anything approaching a chef, when your parents are not in that profession, is practically an impossibility. But at the innocent age of 15, Georges, with his talent and his dreams, began his apprenticeship in a casino hotel near Lyon. He worked long, hard hours with kitchen help that often took advantage of his naïveté and, as Georges puts it, could be very "nasty." But he stuck to it and put in three years toward achieving the career he had chosen; he was proud of himself on returning home and on sharing some of the dishes he learned to make during his apprenticeship. When he prepared one of these dishes, he recalls his father's recommending a little more of this and maybe a little less of that, but it seemed to come across in a constructive, "striving-for-more" manner. After his three-year entry apprenticeship, Georges took a position in the south at Les Baux de Provence under a master chef by the name of Baumanière who could be very demanding, a trait to which young Georges had become accustomed. Monsieur Baumanière had a fine reputation of training some of the best chefs in France, and Georges learned a great deal from his tutelage. While working and learning in Provence, he met a young American, Peter von Starck, who had also revealed himself as a talented apprentice. At that time it was considered a fluke for an American to be accepted into a three-star restaurant in France, where the passion for perfection in matters of cuisine was serious business. Although they were never close friends, Peter was the man who would later play such a pivotal role in Georges's life. With two years under chef Baumanière's tutelage, our young, talented would-be chef attempted to secure a position at the famed restaurant La Pyramide, near Lyon. He was offered and accepted the position at La Pyramide and, most importantly, his talent was recognized and appreciated; but there was little room to advance because of his lack of seniority and his young age. One night after leaving work at the restaurant, he caught sight of Peter walking along the street, and the two of them renewed their acquaintance and repaired to a local brasserie to drink themselves into a pleasant oblivion. As Georges tells it later on, the restaurant business absorbs all your energies and concentration, most especially when there is a conscientiousness aimed at perfection, and this fateful meeting of the two must have been a much-needed break to unwind. Shortly thereafter, Peter came to offer Georges the dream that he had held in his mind and soul since the beginning; he offered him the position of chef in a restaurant that he was to open in Philadelphia called La Panetière. This mind-reeling opportunity was an offer Georges could not refuse, and in view of the sheer difficulty of becoming a sous-chef, much less a chef, in his homeland, he accepted Peter's

La reine, Marie Antoinette, continues to hold court at Le Bec-Fin

offer; so in 1966, Georges Perrier came to America and in the tradition of so many of his compatriots of the past, he came to Philadelphia.

In France, Georges was told how difficult it would be to be a chef in the United States because of the lack of the right, fresh herbs and the good poultry and meats which were so readily available in his homeland. With this advice and a grain of *sel*, Georges and Peter opened La Panetière in the 1300 block of Spruce Street. The restaurant was tiny, only nine tables, but it accorded a certain intimacy with the kitchen and, by extension, an intimacy between guest and chef. Georges worked very hard to bring his experience of food preparation to its highest expression, and after three years he wanted to be on his own to bring about the realization of his passionate drive for perfection. He and Peter parted on good terms; Peter moved to larger quarters and Georges renamed *his* new restaurant Le Bec-Fin. Well, it is certainly no secret that Le Bec's reputation

"Rouge" on Rittenhouse Square

grew rapidly to the point that lines would begin to form early every evening to await one of the nine tables in what was to become an extraordinary adventure in the preparation and enjoyment of food. Georges would often invite the people who were waiting in line into the kitchen so that they might enjoy the steps in the preparation for the evening's menu selections, and with his offerings of wine and his convivial warmth, he would expand the good will and intimacy he hoped to convey in his new restaurant.

The misgivings of his countrymen as to obtaining the right, fresh herbs and the good meats and poultry were answered by people in the area who understood Georges's devotion to excellence and approached him with these special ingredients that they grew or raised, as they, too, shared a passion for things *de la cuisine*. Georges, in turn, helped these new suppliers with the right feeds and seeds, and before long he was able to create his *spécialités* with the ingredients which were *nécessaire* to the preparation of his superb dishes. This graciousness on the part of Philadelphians and those from the surrounding area is a very real quality which I have come to know many times in my intrusiveness to snap my pictures or to gain entry to some secured site; a polite verbal request from me is usually met with a genuine feeling of welcome instead of one of grudging permission. And as the reader may recall, this area is one of exceptional agricultural luxuriance; this agricultural cornucopia might even explain, to some degree, the largesse of the people of the Delaware Valley in some kind of socio-agricultural theory.

In 1983, Georges made the big move to the 1500 block of Walnut Street, and together with his devotion to excellence in food preparation and presentation, he created an ambiance of the *ancien régime* which is special in itself: Louis XVI chairs that are as comfortable as they are elegant and beautiful chandeliers and sconces which showcase his culinary glories. Georges was proud and nervous at the opening, but it would appear that he had been born under a lucky star in many ways. He moved to his new location just at the right

time to greet the era of the free-spending '80s, and he became the successful pioneer whose efforts proved the idea that haute cuisine could flourish in Philadelphia. *Condé Nast*, *Zagat* and *Esquire* magazine were exceedingly generous in their praise of Le Bec-Fin, and the suburban swells began returning to the city to experience this new phenomenon. As a direct result of his accomplishment, other fine restaurants began to follow suit and establish themselves within the city, and Georges became one of the pivotal figures in the renaissance that Center City Philadelphia was about to enjoy. With the opening of the new Convention Center on Arch Street and the constant efforts of Mayor Ed Rendell to revitalize Center City, Philadelphia began to ride a new wave of growth and tourism which has continued to the present and has even generated a second wave of elegant restaurants, some of which were started by those working in the kitchens and dining areas of the first wave. They, too, have been distinguished in the culinary guides on a national level. And so much of the initial impetus, the reintroduction of fine cuisine into Center City Philadelphia, is due to this talented, young Frenchman who showed that it could all be done.

Today there are French outdoor cafés, French bistros and brasseries, and French coffeehouses where the warm aroma of the French roast invites the passerby with a "come hither" summons; there are French bakeries turning out their baguettes, croissants and brioches and Caviar Assouline for the champagne, caviar and truffles set. Add to all this the new high-rise French hotel, Sofitel—with its own brasserie, by the way—and visitors to Philadelphia can immerse themselves in all the amenities of "La Vie en Rose" with lodgings as well as all the great French cuisine which is right here at hand within the city.

The new Ritz-Carlton Hotel

Mansard

5 The Mansards

At the beginning of the 17th century, France was on the road to becoming the most powerful country in Europe. The largest population and a growing, strong, centralized government united around the figure of the king were the elements which were bringing this about. But the arts and architecture at this time were a different story.

Although 16th-century France had successfully assimilated the spirit of the Italian Renaissance, toward the year 1600, the wars of religion (the Reformation and the Counter-Reformation) had dried up much of the country's creative spirit so that for the first half of the 17th century, French art and architecture found itself without direction. Much of the great art of the Italian Renaissance was still centered upon the Church and the best French artists during this period worked outside the country, leaving an artistic void at home which awaited something new. In Italy, Spain and the Germanic countries Renaissance art had begun to evolve into the highly orna-mental styles of the Baroque and the Rococo, but France took an entirely different architectural turn over the first half of the 17th century.

With greater political consolidation of the monarchy in the mid-17th century came the institution of the Royal Academies of the different arts, including architecture. Louis XIII and Louis XIV, togeth-

er with their astute ministers, fostered the development of these Academies both as an aesthetic advancement and as a cultural reflection of the power and majesty of France to the rest of the world. Architectural forms and ideas were now studied and discussed among the Academy members. The result was the development of a refined variant of Renaissance architecture which was distinctively French. This French classicism, once defined, would set a new standard of elegance in architecture and would continue to blossom throughout the next 150 years, and again in the period of the Second Empire. The new defining spirit of this French classicism was best represented by the work of the architect François Mansart (1598–1666), whose elegant architectural renderings of houses, churches and châteaux with high-pitched roofs, graceful, narrow chimneys and metal finials resting upon simple, stone facades of classic orders, all in harmonious proportion, stand in complete contrast to the evolving, highly ornamental Baroque and Rococo styles in the rest of Europe at this period. This French classicism, which found its quintessential expression in the great châteaux of the 18th century, reappeared in the mid-19th century in the form of the Second Empire style and remained a powerful influence not only in France, but also in the rest of Europe and the Americas as a paragon of the elegant expression of the classics. On appreciating Mansart's design for the château of Maisons-Laffitte (1642–1650), situated on the Seine northwest of Paris, it takes little effort to see the striking similarity of the basic design of our City Hall to this landmark structure built more than 200 years before in France. But before going further, let's take a brief look at Monsieur Mansart himself.

François Mansart was born in Paris in 1598. His father had been a master carpenter who died when François was still a young boy, so that his career training as an architect came from a brother-in-law who had worked with Salomon de Brosse, a classical architect of fine repute. Although he never had the opportunity to visit Italy, the young François had such a strong feeling for his calling that he was instinctively able to master the architectural essence of the Italian classics without traveling abroad or receiving any formal training.

Mansart's precocious talent was such that at the age of about 25, he was receiving commissions as an established architect to modify three important buildings, one of which was the château of Balleroy, near Bayeux on the Normandy coast, home to the famous tapestry of 1077, celebrating William the Conqueror's invasion of England. Here at Balleroy, Mansart combined his feeling for classic symmetry with techniques from the time of Henri IV, who reigned as king about thirty years before. His use of rough, brownish-yellow local stone together with quoins (building corners) and window-surrounds of a dressed white stone gave the building a handsome two-toned effect. Two pavilions standing apart from the main building flank the anterior aspect of the château and create an image which is strikingly similar to the two dependencies which flank our beautiful Mount Pleasant in Fairmount Park. At Mount Pleasant, built in the mid-18th century, local brick forms the quoins which dramatically contrast with the wall of white block that appears as masonry; the elegant roof forms a modified mansard, and all is in perfect symmetry to emphasize its classical design. Mount Pleasant was built by an enterprising Scotsman, Captain John MacPhearson, who had gained his fortune as a privateer. The Scots seemed very well disposed to employing French designs for their buildings, especially here in America, as will also be seen by John McArthur, Jr.'s design for City Hall a hundred years later.

The work at Balleroy gave Mansart the important access to Gaston, Duke of Orléans, who was Louis XIII's brother, and afforded him the commission to create the Orléans wing of the château at Blois. Blois (pronounced "Bwa"), one of the most historic châteaux in France, was initially built by King François I in the early 16th century as an expression of the Renaissance movement just beginning to blossom in Italy. Mansart's commission to create a new wing was a high honor indeed, and he worked assiduously to design one which was to become a pinnacle of the new French classicism. His genius literally "takes wing" at Blois and appears to combine a seemingly paradoxical clarity with subtlety, restraint with richness, Renaissance order with flexibility and an aesthetic concentration heretofore unseen in French architecture. But it is the château of Maisons-Laffitte, northwest of Paris (built between 1642 and 1650), that will serve as the more precise model for our City Hall, as well as so many other buildings throughout the world which resonate with the exquisite beauty and dignity of the French Renaissance.

Mansart put together everything he had been elaborating within his craft for years at Maisons, and it is the perfect introduction to the exuberant Second Empire style of our City Hall. The courtyard,

Balleroy. Compare the tiny pavilions flanking the main building with the dependency at our Mount Pleasant.

Dependency at Mount Pleasant
(Fairmount Park)

which was generally absent in the new châteaux, seems to be suggested here from an anterior view of the structure with a gradual envelopment in the approach to the main building. There is a gradation in the height of the wings from the approach and then swinging around into the frontispiece, or the central pavilion encasing the main entrance. This gradation in height is further accentuated by the subtle use of different architectural maneuvers best seen in the main entrance. If we take a close look at the entranceway of the château, we can more fully appreciate Mansart's subtle genius, and at the same time we can see this genius reflected in the creation of our own City Hall.

Château of Maisons-Laffitte

The main entrance at Maisons is composed of three tiers designed to create a crescendo of height and a feeling of greater importance in this central section of the building. To effect this more fully, Mansart employed a progression of the three classical Greek orders from the ground; that is, Doric capitals on the first story, Ionic capitals on the second story and Corinthian capitals on the top. The entablature (the horizontal beam above and across the tops of the columns and capitals) is solid at ground level, with an indentation on the second level and completely broken (or open) at the top level; this accentuates the heightening effect. At the same time, the ornamentation on the lower tier is seen to be centralized above the door with a progressively wider placement and more complexity in design in the two tiers above. The top story is flanked by two sets of urns and a balustrade; and all this is framed with an elegant mansard roof and topped by an additional panel and small cupola which were popular Renaissance additions and which presaged the more stylistic curvilinear mansard roof of the Second Empire and later Beaux Arts styles. The overall effect is one of supreme harmony and richness of detail without an overabundance of embellishments.

Before we take a look at City Hall, there is an additional stylistic trend which deserves consideration at this time. Although France was quick to emulate the classic design of the Italian Renaissance, toward the end of the 16th century there arose in Italy a tendency to

Château of Maisons-Laffitte

*Classical elegance à la Beaux-Arts
(Curtis Institute of Music)*

adorn the classic forms of antiquity with ornate embellishments. This tendency was called the Mannerist style and employed the use of allegorical heads, Cupids, acanthus leaves and vines—all carved into the stone. Mannerism tended to push aside some of the symmetry of Renaissance design by placing these embellishments off-center or by elongating human figures to deprive them of any rational proportion. This trend can be noted in the Curtis Institute of Music, Locust and 18th Streets, where classic Renaissance windows give way to beautiful, round-arched windows with elegant vegetation carved into the arch and cornucopias into the lower panel.

A classical, rounded arch with Mannerist fineries, at the Curtis Institute of Music on Locust Street

These delicate adornments beam with notes of refinement, as does the Curtis Institute itself. Founded in 1924 by Mary Louise Curtis, whose father was the highly successful magazine publisher and founder of the Curtis Publishing Company, the Curtis Institute is one of the most renowned music schools in the world. The original faculty included Josef Hofmann, Leopold Stokowski, Efrem Zimbalist and Leopold Auer. Some of its more celebrated alumni include Leonard Bernstein, Gian Carlo Menotti, Ned Rorem, Samuel Barber, Anna Moffo, Vincent Persichetti and Gary Graffman.

But to return to the building arts, Mannerism could be thought of as a transitional period which eventually gave way to the highly ornamental Baroque and Rococo styles in Italy, Spain and the Germanic countries. There was also some Mannerist influence in France, but Mansart's countercurrent of a studied, more refined Renaissance style really set the tone for the time and gave the world an architecture of such distinction, dignity and grace that it would serve as a model for the great châteaux at home and for many important government and private buildings abroad. In the late 19th century, the mansard roof became so ubiquitous that *any* building or house with the slightest pretense to grandeur had to be capped by one. This overlay of Mannerist detail is important, though, when we look at the Second Empire style of Napoléon III in the last half of the 19th century. The architecture of the Second Empire took the classical Renaissance style as its foundation and with an exuberance of Mannerist detail and certain stylistic variations, especially in the mansard roof, blossomed precisely at the time that Philadelphia was leading the country in industrial development and had become the focus of national and international attention through the Centennial Exhibition in 1876.

The cornerstone for our City Hall was laid in 1871 and the building itself was completed about thirty years later. Philadelphia had become a vibrant force in the new era of industrialization and big business had come to wield a powerful force in a city which had already served as the political and social beacon for the country a century before. A vote was taken to determine the location for the new City Hall, and as if William Penn himself had voiced his opinion, the clear, popular choice was Centre Square at the intersection of Broad and Market Streets where our founder had originally set aside land to serve for the public good 200 years before. The city's emerging importance in the business world, her grand social achievements with so many of the country's "firsts" and the extreme pride Philadelphians had for their city commanded that an especially dignified, beautiful building become the showcase for the new

Our "Hôtel de Ville" dominates Market Street (City Hall)

City Hall. And it was the dignified, refined style of the Second Empire which commanded such authority.

The comparison of Mansart's château of Maisons-Laffitte with our City Hall is at once striking even without considering the finer details, but let us compare the frontispieces of the two buildings. As in Maisons, City Hall has three tiers of classic orders which form the entranceways into the central courtyard. Although Maisons and the great châteaux of 18th-century France had dispensed with the inner courtyard, City Hall retains it for the obvious requirement of space and there are four entranceways which are similar and placed at the center of each side. Here, as in Maisons, the Doric order is employed on the ground level, with the Ionic and Corinthian orders on the second and third tiers, respectively. The orders are overlaid with Mannerist detail, which tends to make them less obvious at first, but this technique can be seen to be the same as that used by Mansart in Maisons. The entablatures progress, as they do at Maisons, with greater recesses and different ornamentation within the frieze areas so that a more subdued, classic motif on the ground level gives way to a Mannerist-style garland on the second tier and a pediment with the city emblem denoting peace and prosperity filling the third tier. Above the curvilinear arch of the third level is an ornate dormer window set into the mansard roof with figures, called caryatids, serving as columns holding up the entablature of the dormer window. The figures facing the south side are African; the figures on the east side are Asian; those on the north side are Norsemen (Caucasian); and those on the west are American Indians. This depiction of peoples from the four corners of the globe was intended as a tribute to the many different cultures which contributed to the city's greatness, and also accentuated William Penn's idea of all people living together in harmony here within the City of Brotherly Love. The traditional mansard with its ornate dormers is framed by a more stylized mansard of the Second Empire era with a curved roof line and rounded windows (called opera windows) much in vogue during this era and set into the flanks of the stylized mansard. City Hall has a wealth of allegorical statuary and ornamentation—more than 200 statues in all. But within the frontispiece there is a progressive centralization of these embellishments as we ascend the tiers. Unlike Mansart's placement of ornamentation at Maisons, City Hall's embellishments come to a crescendo in the ornate dormer windows of the mansard, with the use of differing caryatids, and actually emphasize the form and direction of the roof itself.

City Hall was designed by John McArthur, Jr., and its abundant statuary was the work of Alexander Milne Calder—two noble Scotsmen who contributed much to Philadelphia history. Alexander Stirling Calder, Milne Calder's son, created the dramatic and beautiful statuary which graces the fountain in Logan Circle, and *his* son, Alexander Calder—without the middle name—is world-famous for his unique mobiles which hang in the Parkway entrance to the Philadelphia Museum of Art. A dynasty of sculpting Calders and their works—all to be found within the expanse of the Benjamin Franklin Parkway from City Hall to the Art Museum. Actually, Milne Calder was City Hall's first inhabitant; he set up his studio in the new building's basement in 1875, and began to create more than 200 clay molds of allegorical, historical and geographical figures that were subsequently translated into stone. City Hall was virtually "dripping" in statuary. As for John McArthur, City Hall was, far and away, his most celebrated work. McArthur had been a civil servant at every level of government—local, state and federal; his political career and his service to the Union during the Civil War as an architect who built temporary hospitals and other important structures at the Frankford Arsenal easily won him the commission to design Philadelphia's principal public building, and he put all his efforts into the project.

One of the most dramatic buildings in Center City, 1420 Chestnut Street is just one block away from City Hall. Built in 1898, and originally known as the American Baptist Publication Society, 1420 Chestnut is a glorious rendition of late French Renaissance architecture with Mannerist detail. If the French had had the technology to build skyscrapers back in the 16th century, this is how they might have appeared. The elegant window encasements show slight ornamental variations on their flanks as we look to the upper tiers: there are two *cartouches* (medallions) at the lowest level with recesses and

1420 Chestnut Street

statuary (no longer intact) on the second level and huge *volutes* (scrolls) to provide added grace on the top tier. There is an ordered series of scallop shells just below the roof line, which was a popular Renaissance motif throughout Europe; the scallop shell (or cockleshell), associated with the shrine of Saint James (Santiago) of Compostela in northwestern Spain, may have been significant as a symbol for the Catholic Counter-Reformation besides being an attractive decoration. As can be readily appreciated, the basic elements are all harmoniously symmetrical in true Renaissance fashion, but the ornamentation to the left of the window on the lowest level is indicative of the Mannerist style of the late 16th century with its rebellion against complete symmetry. The bronze finials at the top of the roof are in the shape of miniature Eiffel Towers. All in all, this building is a visual delight which is most unexpected when first seen, but it makes for a dramatic image *à la française* when viewed from Market and 15th Streets, so that City Hall, 1420 Chestnut and the top of the magnificent Bellevue with its stupendous mansard roof follow the line of vision on looking south.

The Bellevue Hotel, built between 1902 and 1913, has been called the most beautiful hotel in America by a number of architects. It has been the "stopping place" for every President since Teddy Roosevelt.

The magnificent Bellevue Hotel

A magnificent structure of classical French Renaissance design, the Bellevue is considered a Beaux Arts masterpiece, along with our Art Museum, the Curtis Institute of Music and so many other fine buildings about town. The term "Beaux Arts" simply means "fine arts" and refers to the School of Fine Arts in Paris. Not long after the influence of the Second Empire style had reached its height, there came onto the scene the so-called Beaux Arts style which was really an eclectic reworking of classical, Romanesque, Gothic, Byzantine and Egyptian styles so that the distinctive features of each were monumentalized to increase their dramatic effects. This made for some exceptionally striking buildings which could be awe-inspiring even without an understanding of their technicalities. At the same time, the Gothic and Romanesque Revival styles were very popular in the design of both civil and ecclesiastical buildings. As the center for art and design, Paris continued to exert her influence both directly and indirectly through the many architects who traveled there to study at the École des Beaux Arts.

At the top of the Bellevue, a curvilinear mansard of exceedingly grand scale is complemented by a large, rounded-arch window with just enough ornamentation to dignify the total image without overpowering it. The small, wrought-iron balcony emphasizes the increasing use of this material in late-19th- and early-20th-century buildings to add a certain dimension of grace to the whole. All in all, the design and the materials convey a harmonious statement of the French Renaissance. The Broad Street facade of the Bellevue displays the original splendor of this magnificent building with balconies, niches, dormer windows and the more traditional mansard roof at either extreme.

When speaking of the Beaux Arts style, the names of two architects come immediately to mind: Horace Trumbauer (1868–1938) and his protégé, Julian Francis Abele (1881–1950). Like François Mansart himself, Horace Trumbauer was a small, retiring man with little formal training in the architectural arts, but one who deeply felt

Classical French Renaissance (a Trumbauer townhouse on Locust Street)

his calling. Although he was never able to attend the École des Beaux Arts, he was considered by many architects as one of the best interpreters of the Beaux Arts style. The Philadelphia Museum of Art, the Curtis Institute of Music, the Philadelphia Free Library on Logan Circle, the Irvine Auditorium on the campus of the University of Pennsylvania, inspired by Mont Saint-Michel on the Normandy coast—Trumbauer and Abele played major roles in the design of all these notable structures. And like Mansart, Horace Trumbauer had the favor of the city's well-to-do and received numerous commissions for country estates and townhouses which, for the most part, were carried out in the classical style of the late French Renaissance.

An "Arc de Triomphe" above Market Street's Reading Terminal (Beaux Arts style)

A robust mansard in Center City (St. James Apartments, Walnut Street)

These Trumbauer buildings in the city and in the suburbs are the personification of grace and refinement.

Julian Francis Abele was the first African American to graduate from the University of Pennsylvania's architectural school and the first African American to attend the École des Beaux Arts in Paris, which sprang from his immeasurable talent and from Trumbauer's enthusiastic sponsorship. Abele joined the Trumbauer firm in 1906 and after his advanced training, he rose to chief designer with contributions to such notable buildings as the Union League addition on 15th Street, the Widener Building at Chestnut and Juniper Streets, the Philadelphia Free Library on Logan Circle, the Irvine Auditorium on the Penn campus and our *pièce de résistance*, the

Our Art Museum
(a Beaux Arts masterpiece)

Philadelphia Museum of Art. These structures are all considered examples of the Beaux Arts style and draw their inspiration from classical, Renaissance, Romanesque, Gothic and Byzantine sources.

Our Art Museum, besides being one of the world's great repositories of art, is also a majestic building in itself. Without any appreciation for architectural details, it is at once clear that this is a visual phenomenon. Perched upon a bluff above the Schuylkill, which William Penn referred to as his "Faire Mount," the Museum commands a special vantage point to give it conspicuous visibility from several approaches into Center City. Not only does it capture the eye with its dramatic grace and beauty, but it also accords a special distinction to our metropolis which lets the beholder know right away that this is not just another American city we are approaching, but the City of Philadelphia. Because of its powerful design and its magnificent setting, it may very well be considered the most beautiful art museum in the world, and I am far from a majority of one in believing this. Its omnipresence, even on the drive home after a hard day's work, often has the compelling effect of reminding me to remember the glory of the spirit instead of dragging home some of the more mundane, crass occurrences of the workplace which have a tendency to haunt us on the way home.

There are some other spectacular buildings in Philadelphia which are considered to be in the Beaux Arts style: the Fidelity Mutual Life Building, one block away from the Art Museum; 1500 Walnut Street; the Packard Building at 15th and Chestnut Streets; 30th Street Station; the Girard Trust Company, now the Ritz-Carlton Hotel across from City Hall; Reading Terminal at 11th and Market Streets; the Rodin Museum at 22nd Street and the Parkway; and the St. James Apartments at 12th and Walnut Streets. To be acquainted with these buildings is to enjoy some of the most exquisite architectural achievements produced in this country.

The glorious simplicity of the Romanesque (St. Clement's on 20th Street)

6 The French Gothic

The Middle Ages produced two distinct forms of architecture in Europe known as the Romanesque and the Gothic. The first style, the Romanesque, originated from the design of the monastery of Cluny in eastern France, and its period of proliferation to the rest of Europe and Asia Minor extended from about 1000 to 1250 A.D. Toward the millennium year 1000 A.D., Christians began to view the Church as the only unifying force in their world at a time when there were no strong central governments. In particular, a need was felt for Christian unity in the face of Islamic conquests and consolidation. The Church began to assume this responsibility for unity and attempted to further it through the institution of three new strategies: the first was the development of a new and beautiful architectural focus to which the faithful could relate, even if they traveled away from home on pilgrimage; the second was the adoption of the Latin rite for the Mass; and the third was the use of the Gregorian calendar to standardize the celebration of the feast days. Romanesque architecture was based on the old Roman basilica of antiquity, which incorporated the rounded arch, heavy walls to support the basic building structure, capitals with graphic tracings of Biblical scenes atop their columns and a transept which usually cut across the nave to form a cross when seen from above. This new architecture spread throughout the Christian world from Scandinavia to the

Strawberry Mansion Synagogue, a pure Romanesque building from Sephardic Spain. Aside from its rounded arches and graphic capitals, the color of the stone so vividly reflects the color of the soil of northern Spain. These Romanesque structures served both as houses of worship and places of refuge during the troubled times of the 11th, 12th and 13th centuries.

British Isles and the Iberian peninsula, and along the northern Mediterranean coast into Asia Minor, Armenia and parts of the Holy Land.

Romanesque architecture is striking in its simplicity and very easy to recognize wherever it may be found. It was an architecture which was rooted to the ground; the stone used in its construction seemed to reflect the same coloration as the earth on which it stood. The heavy walls served as the basic support for the structure as well as a fortress in times of need. The rounded arch, however—the hallmark of Romanesque architecture—was a direct borrowing from antiquity. The Romans had come to realize that the rounded arch provided the strongest structural support that could be used. It is truly amazing, in our day, to travel through some of the old cities of Europe and to find bridges, built more than 2,000 years ago by these

The tiny Romanesque chapel of St. Clare Monastery opposite Girard College

ingenious Romans, which continue to serve as main traffic arteries into and out of these historic, old population centers. They all display the rounded arch supported by substantial piers of stone.

The Gothic style, on the other hand, began to evolve in late-12th-century France and could be considered as different from the Romanesque as any two forms of architecture could be. Instead of being rooted to the ground like the Romanesque, the Gothic soars heavenward with the wall support from flying buttresses and piers somewhat removed from the wall itself. This frees up the walls for

Gothic resplendence (St. Mark's Episcopal Church on Locust Street)

the expansive stained glass windows which are so very characteristic of the Gothic. With its characteristically pointed arches, delicate tracery and vaulted ceilings, the Gothic is much more ornate and decorative than the Romanesque. The word "Gothic," by the way, is actually a misnomer; although we think of the word as meaning "Germanic," it was actually applied at a later date to this architectural style to differentiate it from the classical thread of the Romanesque. The Gothic evolved in France without classical precedence.

Here in Philadelphia, we are indeed fortunate to have authentic examples of both the Romanesque and the Gothic styles in our Museum of Art on the Parkway. A number of archways, chapels and even a complete cloister from southwestern France are here for us to experience the "being there" feeling that these wonderful structures afford. And in town, beautiful echoes of both these styles are to be found in civil as well as church buildings. As the city expanded west of 20th Street in the last quarter of the 19th century, new residences and houses of worship were built as part of the Gothic Revival and its near parallel, the Romanesque Revival.

The Gothic flowered until the mid-16th century, when the thrust of the Renaissance was beginning to make itself felt in the arts and architecture of Europe. But toward the latter 15th century, the Gothic lost some of its pure architectural significance and developed into more of a decorative style with French nuances showing a special distinction in the refinement of its traceries and filigrees. Whenever I have chanced upon these elegant evidences of the French Gothic around the city, I become almost dumbfounded to think that these medieval fineries should exist without any great fanfare as adornments to doorways in Center City; they are the embodiment of melodic lyrics worked in stone.

There are two doorways in Center City which graphically depict these phenomena. The Gothic portal at 245 South 17th Street has squared off the pinnacle of its pointed arch, a late French variation which is seen in its authentic form in the Art Museum, and within its arched tympanum is the carving of a child with outstretched hands, presumably a depiction of the Christ Child, whose hands extend over two small dragons, as symbols of heresy. It is bordered on the bottom by a series of scallop shells; the scallop shell (or, more prop-

245 South 17th Street

erly, the cockleshell) was the symbol in medieval art of St. James (Saint-Jacques or Santiago).

It is interesting to note that the Gothic and Romanesque archways and cloister found in our Art Museum were procured from southwestern France, which placed them along the famous pilgrimage route through France to Santiago de Compostela in northwestern Spain. Santiago de Compostela was one of the three great pilgrimage destinations in the Middle Ages, Rome and Jerusalem being the other two. Pilgrims from all over Europe would gather at the Tour Saint-Jacques across from Nôtre Dame Cathedral in Paris to begin their journey of 900 miles to the famous shrine where the remains of the Apostle James were miraculously discovered in the early 9th century. Legend has it that Charlemagne himself was one of the first pilgrims to visit the shrine; later pilgrims included El Cid, Louis VII of France, St. Francis of Assisi, James II of England and Scotland, Marshal Pétain of France and Pope John XXIII.

James and John, the sons of Zebedee, became the first two followers of Jesus in his active ministry. After the Crucifixion in 33 A.D., James went to the Iberian peninsula to spread the Gospel; in 44 A.D., having returned to the Holy Land, he was beheaded because of his fiery evangelism. Legend has it that a ship bringing granite from Iberia to the Holy Land brought the remains of the martyred apostle back to northwestern Spain where they were miraculously rediscovered in the beginning of the 9th century. "Sant-iago" is derived from "Saint Yacov," Hebrew for Jacob, and came down to the English as Iago, and, later, James. It was indeed an auspicious moment to make this discovery as it served as a rallying point for Christendom in the 800-year Reconquest of the Iberian peninsula from the Moors, who had overrun Spain and had even reached the French town of Poitiers in 732 A.D. The political ramifications are all too obvious, but issues of art and architecture were connected to the famous Way of St. James through France, the Pyrénées and across northern Spain.

It was along the Way of St. James, *le chemin de Saint-Jacques*, that the magnificent art forms of the Romanesque, and later of the Gothic, spread into the towns of western France and then into Spain. Remember, the Romanesque and the Gothic styles had both originated in France. But, more importantly, as both these art forms crossed the Pyrénées into Spain, they came under the influence of the beauty of Moorish art which had already permeated the Iberian peninsula.

In the Gothic portal which adorns the Ann Taylor shop on Walnut Street, the elegant pointed arch is filled in with some of the most delicate geometric designs which are suggestive of the beautiful arabesques of Moorish Spain. To me, the overlay of these two great artistic expressions—late French Gothic and Moorish-Arab design—is uncanny and quite dramatic, and it is by means of the Way of St. James that this synthesis was forged. It is notable that the Romanesque and Gothic portals and cloister found in the Art Museum are also from towns along the Way of St. James.

The design for the cloister on display in the Museum is based on that of Saint-Genis-des-Fontaines, from Roussillon in southwestern

Cloister of Saint-Genis-des-Fontaines,
Roussillon, France, in the Museum of Art.
Courtesy of Philadelphia Museum of Art: Purchased
with funds contributed by Elizabeth Malcolm
Bowman in memory of Wendall Phillips Bowman.

France. This is a Romanesque structure with its rounded arches and graphic capitals, but the alternating red and yellow segments within the arches are a direct borrowing from the Arabs, as can readily be appreciated in the forest of arches of the Great Mosque at Córdoba. The so-called Spanish tile roof was also brought to the Iberian peninsula by the Arabs. The Romanesque fountain in the center of the cloister is from the monastery of Saint-Michel-de-Cuxa in the eastern Pyrénées, and it conveys a truly Arabic feeling to this Christian cloister, which would fit just as comfortably into a Moorish courtyard in Granada in southern Spain.

It is unexpected, and thoroughly delightful, to find these late French Gothic portals with their scallop shells and arabesques incorporated into the doorways of a Center City street. So much history and artistic development are suggested by these quiet thresholds of the late French Gothic.

7 The Left Bank—Le Shopping

*N*obody has such *joie de vivre* as the French. They have taken the essentials of life—food and clothing—and made an art form of both. Whether it is dressing up or dressing down, haute cuisine or *libre service*, the French have a way of making it superb. For, in truth, these are the "must haves" in life, and in France they are transformed into nothing less than artistic expressions.

We Americans seem to place more value on the car we drive or the house we live in, but the French center their values on the day's enjoyment of food and on expressing themselves through their dress. Even the English word "food" has too close an association to the word "fodder" to suit me. And how could the word "clothes" ever

"Rive gauche à Philadelphie"
(le shopping)

"Rive gauche à Philadelphie"
(le shopping)

hope to compete with the French word *vêtements*? No, it is a simple reality—the French live more for the day while we Americans are always thinking of strategies to increase our wealth and to manifest this obsession through our personal possessions, like our cars or our houses.

Well, value judgments aside, it is for these reasons that French fashion and French cuisine are so famous throughout the world. And here in Philadelphia, we are indeed fortunate to have the best of both worlds in that French fashion and French cuisine make their presence known throughout the City of Brotherly Love. Whether it is on the left bank—of the Schuylkill, that is—in Manayunk, in Center City or in one of the nearby suburban locales like the King of Prussia Mall, where such elegant boutiques as Hermès or Louis Vuitton are to be found, there are *beaucoup de couture* and *beaucoup de cuisine à la française* here in Philadelphia.

Bibliography

Alden, John R. *A History of the American Revolution.* New York: Alfred A. Knopf, 1969; Cambridge, Mass.: Da Capo Press, 1989. An engrossing political background of the event.

Barré, François, et al. *Hommage à François Mansart, 1598-1666.* Paris: Editions Hervas, 1998.

Bazin, Germain. *Baroque and Rococo.* London: Thames and Hudson, 1964.

Binney, Marcus, and Frederick H. Evans. *The Châteaux of France.* London: Reed Consumer Books, 1994. Mr. Evans was an English photographer who bicycled through areas of the French countryside at the beginning of the 20th century, before the ravages of two world wars and the commercial developments, tourism and urbanization which were to follow. His photographs are accompanied by essays by Marcus Binney.

Blunt, Anthony. *Art and Architecture in France, 1500-1700.* 5th ed. Revised by Richard Beresford. New Haven: Yale University Press, 1999.

Chestnut Hill Historical Society. *Architectural Guide and Map of Chestnut Hill.* Philadelphia: Chestnut Hill Historical Society, 1997.

Durant, Will, and Ariel Durant. *Rousseau and Revolution.* New York: MJF Books, 1967.

_____. *The Age of Napoléon.* New York: MJF Books, 1975. Inestimable classics, both.

Emgarth, Annette H. *French Philadelphia.* Philadelphia: Alliance Française de Philadelphie, 1991.

Franklin, Benjamin. *The Autobiography of Benjamin Franklin.* 1868. Reprint, New York: Dover Publications, 1996.

Goubert, Pierre. *The Course of French History.* London: Routledge, 1991.

Klein, Philip S., and Ari Hoogenboom. *A History of Pennsylvania.* University Park, Pa.: Pennsylvania State University Press, 1973.

Michener, James A. *Iberia: Spanish Travels and Reflections.* Greenwich, Conn.: Fawcett Publications, 1968. Always one of my favorite modern-day authors.